GIUSEPPE ZANINI

The Hamlyn Book of
WHERE

Hamlyn
London · New York · Sydney · Toronto

Contributors:
Andrea Bonanni
Pinuccia Bracco
Glauco Pretto

Published 1974 by
The Hamlyn Publishing Group Limited
London · New York · Sydney · Toronto
Astronaut House, Feltham, Middlesex, England
© Text copyright 1973 Arnoldo Mondadori Editore, Milano
© Text copyright this edition 1974 the Hamlyn Publishing Group Limited
© Illustrations copyright The Hamlyn Publishing Group Limited

ISBN 0 600 39299 6

Printed by Officine Grafiche Arnoldo Mondadori, Verona, Italy

INTRODUCTION

The fascination of distant, mysterious places has always been very much alive in young boys and girls. Thanks to the cinema and television cameras which have investigated every corner of the world, there are few mysteries left to be uncovered.

And yet young people are still fascinated by exotic countries, strange customs and different civilizations. Each day the television screen brings us pictures and details of different parts of the world; and lavishly illustrated geography books and newspaper reports enrich our geographical knowledge. All this information opens up new horizons for us, and shows us how limited our knowledge is, so that we try to acquire further information, discover unknown phenomena and enlarge our experience.

This is why this volume has been dedicated entirely to geography. Its series of brief articles is designed to take boys and girls on a journey around the world. The subdivision of information according to the continents is the only concession made to the geographical structures usually observed in the compilation of a geographical text. Furthermore, this book, which has only one prevalent feature, curiosity, attempts to provide little-known facts and deal with them from unusual angles.

For what age group are these books suitable? This question has no real answer. It is like asking how old you have to be to admire the countryside, or the sunset, or the Galaxy. With the exception, perhaps, of very small children who would have difficulty in understanding the text, we can safely say that these books are suitable for all age groups and can be consulted by children and adults alike. Everyone will find something to interest him, and be able to satisfy his curiosity on a variety of topics.

Other books in this series:

**The Hamlyn Book of When
The Hamlyn Book of Why
The Hamlyn Book of How**

CONTENTS

	PAGE
The Where of Europe	10
The Where of Africa	32
The Where of Asia	56
The Where of North and Central America	82
The Where of South America	108
The Where of Oceania	130
The Where of the Seas and the Oceans	152
The Where of the Polar Regions	162
List of Questions	179

THE WHERE OF EUROPE

Where you can find the most densely populated state

There are thirty-four states which together make up the whole of Europe; and one of these alone, the U.S.S.R., is so big that, even without its Asiatic part, it covers one half of Europe. Of the others, seven are minute: in descending order they are Luxembourg, Andorra, Malta, Lichtenstein, San Marino, Monaco and the Vatican City.

Of these seven, Monaco holds an extraordinary record; it is the most densely populated state in the world. Its territory occupies an area of approximately one and a half square kilometres and its population of about 25,000 averages 17,000 people to every square kilometre. No other state in the world is as thickly populated as this tiny piece of land set on the Côte d'Azur which with its beauty and temperate climate has become an ideal holiday resort.

In addition to its natural beauty, the Principality of Monaco also boasts cultural attractions. The Museum of Oceanography is renowned for its unique collection: very rare, stuffed marine animals; ancient boats; fishing nets of extraordinary size and shape; and every other object which can be related to sea life. The Museum also possesses a beautiful aquarium which houses a splendid selection of marine fauna.

Where shrews live

Shrews are tiny animals which live in moist places in the woods, burrowing into leaf mould in search of their food.

These creatures are often mistaken for mice and yet there are many differences between the two: shrews have a longer snout which juts out beyond the lower lip, and an extremely sharp set of teeth, whereas mice have chisel-like teeth. Furthermore, a shrew has a long, supple tail almost as long as its body, and on its side it has a gland which emits a strong, rather repellant, musky smell which is a means of defence against its enemies.

In spite of their small physique, shrews are ferocious, carnivorous animals, capable of attacking prey larger than themselves. They feed mainly on insects, snails, worms and small mammals and are very active, eating almost continuously.

Where you can find the cork-oak tree

Cork, a material used mainly for bottle-stoppers, insulation and floor coverings, is produced from a special type of evergreen oak tree which grows, sometimes wild, in the coastal regions of the Mediterranean.

The cork-oak has a thick, dark foliage, formed from noded branches, covered with tough, oval leaves which are small and slightly jagged.

Its thick, tall trunk is completely wrapped in an outer bark of cork which is covered with fine brown grooves. The tree is first stripped of its cork, which will be rather hard and knobbly, when it is about sixteen years old. It is then stripped again every nine to ten years, depending on its location, and each time it will produce a good, light cork just over three centimetres thick.

After about 150 years, these trees cease to produce good quality cork and they are then felled.

Where you can find the land of fiords

Inlets, gulfs, indented coastlines can all be found along every coast of Europe and the other continents. The most characteristic, however, are the fiords of the Norwegian coasts and the Polar, Arctic and Antarctic regions.

These are long, narrow arms of the sea, usually extending far inland. They reach depths of more than 100 metres, and some far exceed this; Sognefjord in Norway, for example, is about 1,320 metres deep. Sometimes they have been called 'marine rivers'.

During the Quaternary Era, in the north-western part of the Scandinavian mountains, glaciers thrust down into the sea, and as time went on they carved deep U-shaped valleys in the rocks. The waters of the sea invaded these valleys, forming inlets known as fiords.

Today it is estimated that there are about 1,700 glaciers in Norway and some are still forcing their way ahead until they touch the sea.

The megalithic monument, Stonehenge, near Salisbury. It was built around 1800–1400 B.C.

Where you can find Megalithic monuments

Of all the monuments that the ancient inhabitants of the Earth have left behind as proof of their civilization, the stark magnificence of such constructions as the Egyptian pyramids are often the most striking.

In Great Britain we have typical examples of unadorned monuments, which can be traced back to the Neolithic Age, in the so-called 'henges'. These are circular in form and consist of vast stone blocks arranged in groups. They are surrounded by a bank and beyond this a circular ditch broken by entrance gaps. They can be found in the north of England and in Scotland, but the place most famous for its prehistoric monuments is Stonehenge.

Where the boar lives

Boars, the ancient forefathers of the domestic pig, have long been extinct in Britain but they still live in fairly large numbers in marshy, woodland areas in Spain, Austria, Russia and Germany. Some species can also be found in northern Africa and central and northern Asia.

Because of their great strength, speed and ferocity when at bay boars have always been hunted by man. In some parts of Europe and India they are still hunted, usually with the aid of dogs. They have not died out, however, mainly because they are prolific animals, the female producing between five and eight offspring at a time.

Boars have sociable natures and live in flocks in dense, wooded areas. They feed on acorns, beechnuts, and chestnuts and occasionally small hard-shelled animals, worms, small birds or mice. They even eat serpents, as they are immune to their poison.

In order to get rid of parasites, they wrap themselves in the mud.

Where flying began

Man has always longed to fly. In the late fifteenth century, Leonardo da Vinci was working on the problem of flying and a century later, a Jesuit priest from Brescia in northern Italy, suggested using the ascending force of the lightest gases present in the air. In 1782, the Neopolitan, Tibero Cavallo, filled a balloon with hydrogen and carried out some laboratory tests.

In France, a balloon full of hot air was publicly launched on 4 June 1783 at Annonay by the Montgolfier brothers. Etienne and Joseph. They repeated the experiment with a larger balloon at Versailles on 19 September 1783 when a hen, a sheep and a duck were the first living creatures to go up in a 'Montgolfier balloon'. On 21 November the Marquis of Arlandes and Pilâtre de Rozier, flew across from Paris, on board a hot air balloon.

The following month, December 1783, hydrogen was substituted for hot air. The physicist J. H. C. Charles with M. N. Robert made the first manned flight using hydrogen.

Where you find the home of the mouflons

Mouflons, the founders of the family of domestic sheep, are indigenous to Sardinia, where even today they live in flocks in the arid, rocky mountains of the Gennargentu; they also roam freely in Corsica and the islands of Ponza, off the west coast of Italy.

The mouflon is a large sheep, stocky and robust, living wild on the heights of rugged and secluded mountainous regions. Only the male has long, curved horns.

Where you can find the Alhambra

The tourist who ventures on to the hill dominating Granada, in southern Spain, has the impression that he has stepped into the heart of an Arabic town.

An ancient palace and fortress occupies the entire summit of the hill; it is the Alhambra, which in Arabic means 'the red'. Red is the predominant colour of the citadel, given to it by the bricks made of fine gravel and clay of which the outer walls are built.

Arabian architects and an army of labourers worked from 1238 to 1358, building and embellishing this immense construction which covers an area of 140,000 square metres. But vastness and magnificence are not the sole characteristics: beauty, elegance, pomp and grace are displayed in the halls, courtyards, marble colonnades, arches and fountains which are all features of Moorish art.

The park was planted with roses, oranges and myrtles by the Moors, but it also includes a wood of English elms taken there by the Duke of Wellington in 1812.

Horses from the Parthenon frieze, in the British Museum

Where you can find the friezes from the Parthenon

Between 447 to 438 B.C. the Athenians erected a temple in honour of the goddess Athene, the protectress of their city. They named it the Parthenon, that is a temple dedicated to the virgin (*parthenos*) Athene.

Together with magnificence of construction, purity of classical lines and the austere majesty of the temple, the Parthenon also possessed many sculptures, some the works of the great Phidias. Many of these unique works of art can today be found in the British Museum, in London.

Thomas Elgin, a British diplomat in Athens who was also an archaeological enthusiast, came into possession of many of the sculptures which had adorned the gables and metopes and friezes of the Acropolis of Athene. In 1803 he brought these treasures to London and exhibited them in his home.

Later they were purchased by the British government and today form part of the most priceless treasures of the world's largest museum.

Where the Victorian style was born and flourished

In June 1837 a new queen ascended the throne of England. She was a young woman, just eighteen years old, with a fragile, submissive appearance who was to prove herself a queen of exceptional character, intelligence and ability; whose influence, spreading even beyond the British Isles, characterized an entire historical era. During her sixty-four years' reign, Victoria dominated the political scene to such an extent that even the arts came under her sway.

The Victorian Age, as it was known, was born in Britain and infiltrated the whole of the British Empire (which constituted almost one-third of the world).

In architecture and other forms of art, including furnishings, the Victorian style showed the same uncertainties as the other styles of art which existed in the last decade of the 1800s. The romantic and the classical intermingled, often incapable of expressing themselves with originality.

Three-seated chair of carved walnut, made around 1850

Where the horned viper lives

The horned viper belongs to the reptile family. Dispersed throughout Yugoslavia and some regions of Austria these vipers can also be found in Italy on the eastern Alps. They are easily distinguishable from the usual *vipera aspis* and *vipera berus* by a horn, sometimes growing to a length of 5 centimetres, which sprouts out from the tip of the head.

The horned viper prefers limestone or very stoney ground, and loves hot climates. It moves rather slowly, particularly during the day, when it sits lazily in the sun, digesting its captured prey which it swallows whole. But, if disturbed, the viper rears up emitting a hissing noise and sinking into the flesh of its enemy two poisonous fangs which are normally kept folded and hidden in a sac in its palate. In this respect, its behaviour is quite similar to that of the other European vipers.

Where you can find the vauclusian spring

There exists a type of rock, limestone, which is very permeable and with which water chemically combines, causing it to dissolve and forming deep fissures in the soil. In this way, a deep, intricate network of canals is formed in the subsoil. These subterranean rivers flow on to a platform of impermeable rocks on which a mountain of limestone builds up. If these impermeable rocks form at a level higher than the surrounding soil, a spring will surge up along the points of contact between the two blocks.

Over the centuries, the atmospheric agents have gradually eroded these mountains and have torn away the earth, stones and pebbles from their summits and deposited them on the strata of the mountains. The water travels for a few metres under these deposits (which are quite large) and then gushes out again on the plains, at a point where the clay or other impermeable water-bearing rocks come to the surface.

In this case, the spring is known as a resurgent or 'vauclusian' after the Vaucluse area in south-eastern France where such springs occur. In Italy, on the plain which stretches away at the foot of the large Alpine chain, there are many resurgent springs, and the water, before it reaches the surface, beats a dark passage for itself inside the earth, passing under the elevations in the hills which form a cordon to the south of the Alps, and gushes out, in abundant springs, between the fields. These springs are precious for irrigation and the water is of a constant temperature.

Where the sacred mistletoe ceremonies were held

On the sixth night of the December moon, the large oak forests of Gaul used to witness one of the most mysterious rites of antiquity: the festival of mistletoe. This was a religious ceremony of the Druids, a caste of priests who dominated and controlled all the social activities of the ancient Celts.

They not only exercised their priestly powers but they also appointed leaders and kings, arranged the education of the young, and administered justice. Their most important and feared god was Teutates to whom they offered sacrifices, sometimes even human sacrifices.

One of the major religious centres of the Druids appears to have been the area around Lyons, whose ancient name (Lugdunum) was derived from the name of the god, Lugos.

Since ancient times mistletoe had always been looked upon as a plant of good omen and during the rites at the end of the year, the priests cut the mistletoe from the trees, using a golden sickle, and then distributed the twigs to their followers.

The Druids at their festival of mistletoe

Where you can find the land of the tulips

The tulip is undoubtedly one of the best known and most popular flowers in the world. Its vivid colours and the simple lines make it a small masterpiece, much prized in both gardens and homes.

The ancient origin of the tulip is unknown, but we have much information on its introduction into Europe. It was the Turks who brought this flower to the West some 400 years ago. The name tulip means 'turban' which the flower is thought to resemble.

There is probably no other flower which has been given such an enthusiastic welcome or spread so quickly throughout Europe. Within the space of a few years, the craze for tulips grew into 'Tulipomania', reaching its height in Holland.

Certain rare varieties fetched astronomical prices: by 1610 some tulip bulbs were worth as much as an ale-house or a mill. One bulb was paid for with a new carriage, complete with two horses, another was exchanged for 12 acres of land. Materials and lace were decorated with designs of tulips. This craze lasted for almost half a century.

Although indigenous to hot countries, the tulip also adapts well to colder climates. Today, Holland is universally renowned as the homeland of the tulip. The Dutch became the prime cultivators of this flower which through four centuries of acclimatization in Europe has undergone certain transformations which have given it the structure and colour we know today.

Where the lynx was seen again in Europe

The lynx is a large, wild, feline animal found in many parts of central Europe. It has unusually large paws, a mottled tawny to cream coat and a black-tipped tail.

The lynx lived in the Alps until half a century ago: the last time this creature is known to have been captured was at the beginning of this century, near Chieri in Piedmont. The animal has not been heard of since.

It is more likely to be the clearance of all trees from the mountains which has caused its disappearance than the fact that it has been hunted down. A deer which had been completely ravaged as if by a lynx, was recently found in a Swiss forest, where there were also impressions in the fresh snow which scientists have identified as tracks typical of this feline creature.

It is thought that, in a few years time, the lynx may reappear on the slopes of the Italian Alps. It usually lives in dense forests where it can find its favourite prey, the roe-buck and the stag.

Where you can find the valley of the temples

Beside the town of Agrigento in Sicily is the valley of the temples where, in the days of the Magna Graecia, the people erected sanctuaries in honour of their gods.

'Fairest of mortal cities' as the Greek poet, Pindar, described it, Agrigento was one of the richest and most beautiful towns of ancient times. It was founded in 582 B.C. by settlers from Rhodes and Crete and by others who came from nearby Gela. The region was rich in grain, oil, wine and cattle; as the years went by the town added to its wealth by constructing a spacious boundary wall and magnificent buildings, including some splendid temples.

Very soon, however, its power clashed with that of the Carthaginians. Strongly fortified and allied with the people of Syracuse, Agrigento defeated the Carthaginians in the famous battle of Himera (480 B.C.).

Most of Agrigento's art treasures were destroyed when it was sacked in 406 B.C. during the wars between the Romans and the Carthaginians.

Where you can find the smallest state in the world

Covering an area of less than half a square kilometre the Vatican City is the smallest state in the world.

Approximately half of its territory is occupied by famous constructions: the Basilica of St Peter standing at the head of a large square which is encompassed by Bernini's magnificent colonnade; the Vatican palaces, the residence of the Pope; the Vatican museums, rich in works of art; and the Sistine Chapel. In the remaining area are gardens, shops, squares, a railway station and an astronomical observatory.

St Peter's, with its famous dome by Michelangelo

Where the brown bear lives

A bad-tempered, unsociable type of person is often said to be 'grizzly' like a bear. The bear is, in fact, a solitary, irascible animal which shuns not only the presence of human beings but even avoids close proximity with his own fellow-creatures. It is difficult to find two bears together, except of course for a couple with their offspring.

There was a time when bears were inhabitants of all Eurasian countries as they adapted well to all climates, although they preferred rigorous weather conditions.

Today, the areas of Europe in which the bear has survived are greatly reduced in both number and size. In particular the brown bear now lives in some of the valleys of the Alps (the Genoa valley and the Tovel valley) in the Pyrenees and the Carpathians.

This bear is of a considerable size, although it is not as large as the polar bear or the grizzly bear of Alaska. It can reach a length of nearly 2 metres and a weight of 150 kilogrammes, although the race from eastern Siberia is almost as large as the grizzly bear.

Where you can find crocodiles in Europe

Outside the tropical and sub-tropical regions crocodiles can only be found today in museums and zoological gardens, but in distant times the crocodile also lived in Europe, mostly in the Mediterranean basin.

In the days of the great dinosaurs some land masses such as the Italian peninsula had not yet emerged from the seas, but large islands, surrounded by cliffs which were forming vast lagoons, were surging up around the Alps and the Pre-Alps. The climate was very much hotter than it is today, as a result of which the vegetation was similar to that which is now found in the islands of the South.

There were extensive forests of palm trees and other tropical plants, and a great variety of reptiles crawled through the undergrowth which was teeming with insects. Gigantic turtles periodically crossed the narrow straits of the sea; large serpents, similar to the boa which is today an inhabitant of America, climbed lazily along the branches of the trees; numerous crocodiles were waiting to pounce on any prey which rashly approached the banks of the sea.

As evidence that these crocodiles once lived in Europe, there still exist fossils which can be seen in Bolca in the province of Verona in Italy. In those far off times, Bolca was a lagoon island. Fortunately, the plants and animals populating this island were preserved in a very fine slush which turned to stone; they became fossilized and have reached us today in excellent condition. Amongst these fossils there are some of ancient crocodiles.

Where the ancient town of Spina once stood

In the delta of the river Po, about 7 kilometres west of modern Comacchio, the remains of an imposing cemetery have been found. These have been attributed to the town of Spina which was once situated in that area.

Excavations began in 1922 when drainage of the land unearthed the remains of nearly 2,000 tombs dating back to the sixth century B.C. Many bronzes and a large collection of Greek pottery were discovered.

The town of Spina was the meeting point of two great pre-Roman civilizations, the Grecian and the Etruscan. It was founded as a result of the Etruscan advance into northern Italy at the end of the sixth century B.C. and became a commercial centre for the market of products which had been brought across the Adriatic from Greece. Considered by Hellenic writers as a true Greek town, it was also an important Etruscan centre and, together with nearby Adria and Ravenna, it gave the Etruscans of northern Italy access to the sea.

Spina was a frontier town, born on the spot where there had once been an indigenous village. Its position gave it great importance, from both a commercial and a cultural point of view. A large colony of Greek merchants resided in the town and they were undoubtedly responsible for mingling Greek with Etruscan culture. This brought Italy spiritually closer to the Greek world. This town was, therefore, more than a large market market place: it was a crossroads of civilizations. Soon after 400 B.C. it was sacked by the Gauls and its importance rapidly declined.

Where you can find the home of the bagpipes

Every land is justly proud of its own customs, traditions and products which reveal its individual character.

This is the case with Scotland, which for centuries has been famous for its kilts, bagpipes and whisky as well as for the beauty of its scenery and the history of its people.

Pipers were always part of the regular retinue of the Highland chieftains, and frequently handed on their office from one generation to another. The clan piper still takes an important part in Highland festivities, funerals and other formal occasions. There is a piper at the royal castle of Balmoral and pipers are attached to all the Highland regiments.

It is because of the Scots' love of tradition that processions of pipers are so popular today. Their distinctive dress with the tartan kilts showing the clan to which they belong, are familiar sights on ceremonial occasions.

To play the bagpipes, the piper blows into a tube so that his breath inflates an airtight leather bag. From this bag the air proceeds through three wooden pipes which contain reeds of fixed tone, called drones. It then goes through another reeded pipe, the chanter, which produces the melody.

When playing the piper has the drones over his left shoulder, the bag tucked under his left arm and he holds the chanter with his fingers.

A variety of music, especially marches and dances, have been composed for the bagpipes. Until recently it was written down in a notation of its own, but now ordinary musical notation is used.

Where you can find the fish which produce caviar

The sturgeon, a shark-like, bony fish, is caught mainly for its flesh, which is sold fresh, pickled or smoked, and its eggs, more commonly known as caviar.

It prefers the waters of temperate or cold areas and can be found only in the Northern Hemisphere.

During the breeding season in early summer, large shoals of sturgeon swim into the rivers or towards the shores of freshwater lakes. In Europe sturgeon occur from Scandinavia to the Mediterranean and, in particular, several species are found in the Caspian Sea and the Black Sea.

Where you can find forests full of beech trees

In parts of western Asia and all Europe as far as southern England, beech trees can be found growing in gardens and large avenues.

There are many different kinds of beech, including the dark-leaved copper beech and the weeping beech, often to be seen in parks.

The best beeches are found in chalky soil, some of them reaching from about 30 to 45 metres high. Many were first planted in the eighteenth century on huge estates.

The timber of the beech is heavy and hard and is extremely useful as firewood. It also has many other uses and is especially noted for making fine furniture and all sorts of different wooden articles.

Where the edelweiss grows

Is it true that these splendid flowers only grow on the face of a steep, rocky mountain, facing an abyss, in a virtually inaccessible place?

So many mishaps have befallen the inexperienced mountaineers whose desire to pick an edelweiss has driven them up to the top, that many imagine that this flower only grows on impossible mountain peaks.

In actual fact, the edelweiss grows wherever the soil is calcareous, at an altitude of more than 1,500 metres, and it can also be found at a lower altitude, in the valleys. In certain areas, at more than 2,000 metres, which are rarely visited by man, it is possible to find these flowers growing in open spaces, among the grass.

In easily reached places, however, this flower has been almost completely destroyed by excessive gathering. This is why the edelweiss now only inhabits the almost inaccessible and dangerous parts of the mountain.

This plant can be cultivated in rock gardens and, given ideal conditions, it will produce a very large corolla. It also grows in open country but here its petals tend to lose their hairy protection and assume a greenish colour.

Where you can find a land full of windmills

Since ancient times man has exploited the forces of nature in an effort to obtain from them the greatest possible aid for his work. One of these forces is the wind: caught in the sails of a boat or used for turning the sails of a windmill, it is the workman's oldest tool and a help to human labours.

Today, the country famous throughout the world for its windmills is Holland, a flat, windy country whose people have the reputation of being among the most industrious and enterprising in the world.

For many centuries the characteristic towers of the windmills have made the countryside of the Low Countries quite unmistakable. These windmills have varying forms: rounded and slightly conical, prismatic, pretty, decorative or unadorned. All of them, however, are positioned so as to receive the greatest force of the wind: the sails, which a breath of air will put in motion, rise over them all.

In Holland, windmills are used more for lifting water than for milling grain. In order to drain the land, they are used to pass water from one canal to another and it is in this way that a country which has always been at war with water manages to maintain hydraulic balance.

The commercial centre at Rotterdam

A view of the Doges' Palace

Where you can find the most famous city on water

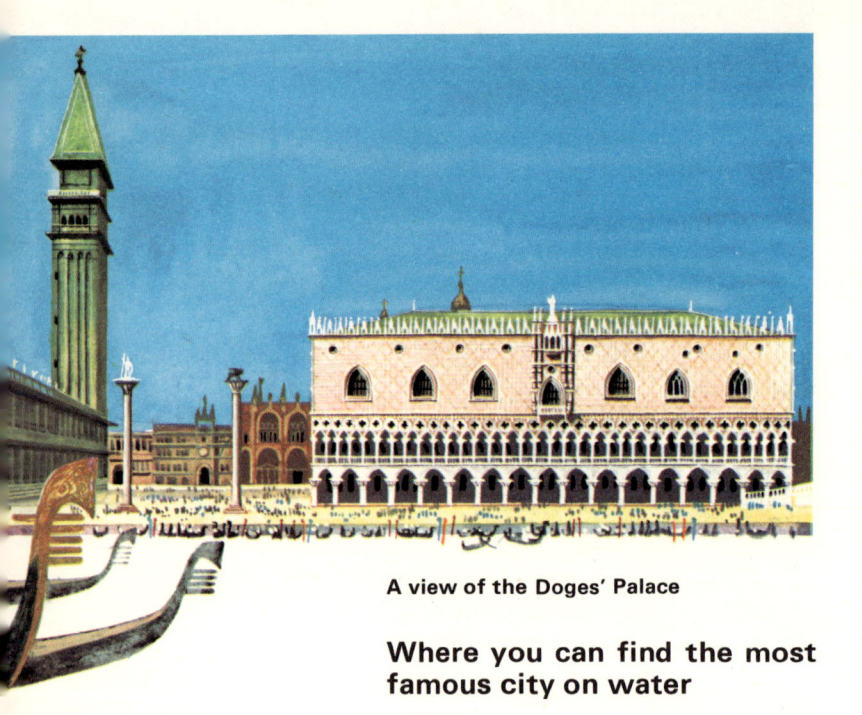

The fame of Venice and its incomparable natural and artistic beauties was confirmed when a world-wide fund was opened to save its treasures. The enormous sums collected show the love felt in every part of the world for this Italian city, set on the water.

Venice is built on about 115 islands in the Adriatic Sea, 4 kilometres east of the mainland to which it is connected by road and rail. The city is intersected by canals, the chief of which is the Grand Canal, and has nearly 400 bridges.

In addition to its canals and bridges, Venice is renowned for its churches and palaces. The most famous of these are St. Mark's Cathedral with its tall campanile beside it built at one end of the Piazza San Marco, and the Doges' Palace.

In the course of the centuries, innumerable artists have been inspired by Venice and in return they have left the results of their creative genius.

Where you can find important Etruscan cemeteries

Many remains of Etruscan civilization have been discovered in central and northern Italy, especially in Tuscany, the northern part of Lazio and Umbria; that is, those areas which were once Etruria.

The Etruscans were great followers of a cult of the dead whom they buried in tombs, some modest, some monumental, according to the social standing of the deceased.

A necropolis, or cemetery, has been discovered in Cerveteri, the ancient Caere. The graves were in rows, divided by paved streets. The larger tombs were hewn in the rock and covered with a small mound of earth.

The subterranean tombs in the necropolis at Tarquinia had actual rooms for each of the dead, and the walls were painted in gay, vivacious colours. The paintings depicted banquets and dances, fights between wrestlers or gladiators, chariot races, jugglers, hunting and fishing; all the activities of a world which disappeared some 2,000 years ago.

Etruscan helmet

Where you can find beautiful marble

Italy has been named the land of marble because of the abundance and variety of the marble found in its mountains.

Italian marble has a vast range of colours: there is the deep black of the Lombardian marble, the pure white of the marble of Carrara, the reds and light yellows of the marbles of Verona and Vincenza, the soft stone colours of the marble of Trani, the clear yellow of the marble of Siena and the golden yellow of the marble of Cuneo.

There are also the various emerald tones of the green, alpine marble and the Ligurian marble from Polcevera, and the blood-red marble with white speckles from the Levant.

Italian marble is exported throughout the world. It has formed in the mountains from strata of marine sediments which have only recently appeared. These limestone sediments, due to the action of the heat and enormous pressures, have assumed a crystalline structure and they have been transformed into marble. Diversity of colour is due to the presence of various mineral substances.

Ancient civilizations were situated in places where true marble was scarce, which is why the most ancient monuments were constructed from other stones or from clay bricks. The first full-scale use of marble in architecture occurred in Greece, where this material was greatly valued for statues and buildings. From Athens the use of marble spread to Rome and then through the whole world.

Where you can find the land of the sunflower

Sunflowers with their round golden heads are grown in gardens where their beauty can be admired, and in fields where they are planted for their seeds.

In Europe the largest habitat of the sunflower is in the Ukraine, a region of the Soviet Union where the black soil is rich in nutritive substances which are ideal for this type of cultivation.

Immense expanses of golden heads, whose diameters sometimes reach 30 centimetres, and of stalks growing to a height of 4 metres, cover kilometre after kilometre of fertile plain, providing a spectacle which is at once vivid and imposing.

A native of North America, the sunflower leaves can be used as fodder for animals, the flowers provide a yellow dye, and oil suitable for industrial use and for foodstuffs is extracted from its seeds. It is no coincidence that the sunflower is cultivated in regions where olives and other oil producing plants are scarce.

Where you can find the remains of ancient human settlements in northern Europe

The most ancient settlers came to northern Europe between 5000 and 4000 B.C. in the Neolithic Age and established themselves in the regions which today correspond to Poland and Germany.

The Danubian culture reached Germany and the Netherlands and was widespread at about 4000 B.C. The people lived in fairly large villages of rectangular timber houses. Remains have been found of their pottery, decorated with incised spiral patterns.

The Ellerbek culture, as it became known, flourished at a later date and there exist many interesting items belonging to this period: wooden hoes, vases with a conical base and ceramic oil lamps.

Another Neolithic culture in Europe is the one characterized by its beakers with funnel necks which, in 3500 B.C., spread from Holland as far as Poland.

Neolithic shelter, Norway

Where you can find the most famous natural grottoes in Europe

The celebrated grottoes of Postojna are situated in a karst field in West Slovenia, Yugoslavia. Tortuous galleries, caves, magnificent rooms richly decorated with stalagtites and stalagmites stretch for nearly 30 kilometres. It is here that the river Pivka flows along in one of the most fantastic subterranean beds in the world.

The grottoes of Postojna have been famous since 1213: engraved in one wall you can read the signatures of people who visited the grottoes as long ago as 1250. But the caves were unknown in modern times until 1818.

Today, tourists can visit the caves in a small electrified railway. Among the most celebrated are the Concert Hall, the Ballroom and the Paradise Grotto.

The remains of a cremation from the Iron Age, found in Finland

Where Palladio's art is supreme

The most famous architect of the Renaissance is Andrea di Pietro, named Palladio by his patron, Trissino.

Born in Padua in 1508, he spent most of his working life in Vicenza. After lengthy preparation in Rome, he planned and built his first great monumental work: the town hall in Vicenza, known as the Basilica. Here Palladio erected a two-storey arcade of white stone around three sides of the mediaeval Hall of Reason (Sala della Ragione).

Also in Vicenza, he designed the Loggia del Capitano which remained incomplete and the Teatro Olimpico which was constructed after his death.

His work on private buildings was of even greater renown; his villas and palaces are famous and although he built so many they were all original: Chiericati, Thiene, Valmarena, Barbarano and Capra palaces are amongst his most famous: the villas of Bagnolo and of the Foscari family called La Malcontenta and the Rotonda built on the Monte Berico are noteworthy.

The works of Andrea Palladio can also be seen outside the town and province of Vicenza, but he always built within the region of Veneto.

The churches of S. Giorgio Maggiore and Il Redentore at Venice are the most well-known of his more important constructions.

The Public Buildings of Udine, the Fratta Villa in the delta of the river Po and the Maser Villa in the province of Treviso are further examples of the works which Palladio has left to us.

Where sleighs are still being used as taxis

It seems impossible that in the age of the motor vehicle there are still places where animal traction is used for public transport.

This is the case in some parts of Switzerland, for example between Zermatt and Taesch, where transport during the winter months is by horse-drawn sleighs. It is like taking a leap into the past, when noise and pollution were almost unknown words.

During the summer, transportation of passengers and goods is carried out by battery-operated locomotives which are completely silent and so do not disturb the calm of the valley.

The Chiericati Palace

Where the Neanderthal Man used to live

The term Neanderthal refers to a type of *homo sapiens* who was already notably civilized. He knew how to clothe himself he could use the hand-axe, he went hunting with sharpened weapons made of flint and he knew how to make a fire which was particularly useful in driving bears away from the caves in which he wished to live.

The name is derived from the Neanderthal valley in Germany where the first skeleton which could be traced back to these times was found. Other discoveries have revealed that Neanderthal people also lived in France, Italy and Belgium.

(1) Swanscombe
(2) Channel Islands
(3) Spy
(4) La Chaise
(5) La Cave
(6) Le Moustier
(7) La Ferrassie
(8) Martmaurin
(9) La Chapelle aux Saints
(10) Malarnaud
(11) Neanderthal
(12) Steinheim
(13) Gánovce
(14) Sipka
(15) Krapina
(16) Marte Circeo
(17) Gibraltar
(18) Kiik Koba
(19) Mt Carmel
(20) Teschik-Tasch
(21) Broken Hill
(22) Saldanha

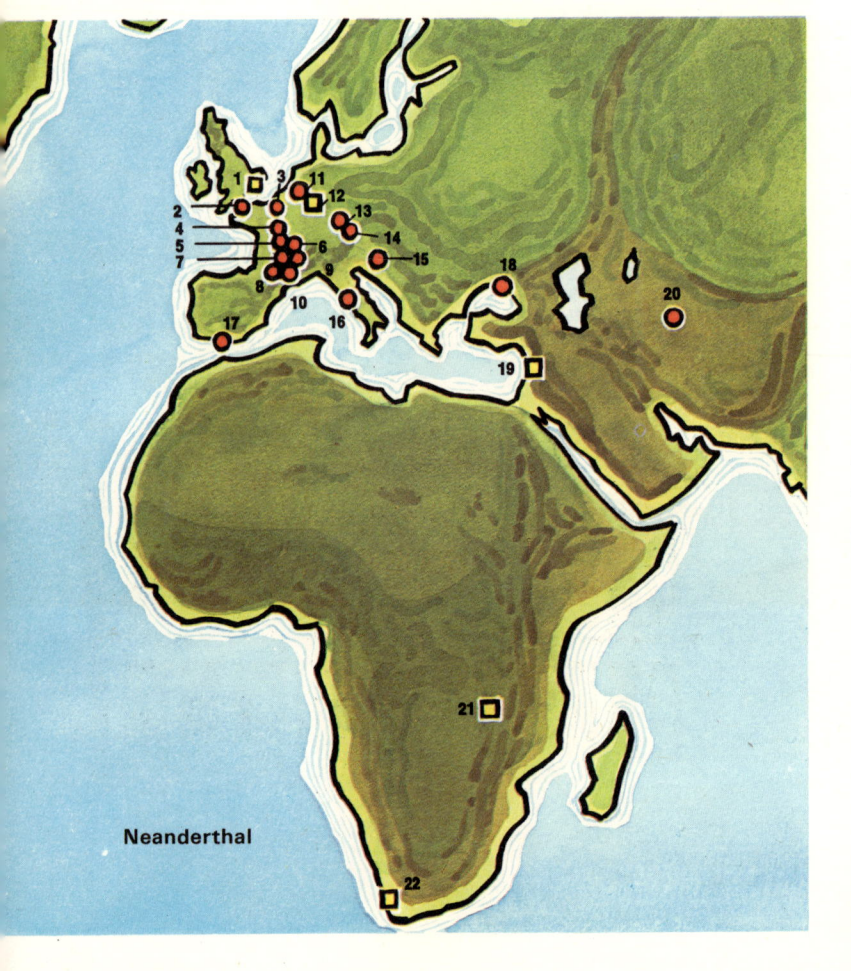

Where orchids grow in Europe

The name orchid usually evokes a picture of dense forests covered with a lush vegetation, where these marvellous tropical flowers prosper and bloom amongst ancient trees. In fact, the most precious orchids, today cultivated in greenhouses, come from distant regions where the climate is hot or humid.

But beautiful orchids also grow naturally in Europe. Their small flowers are not particularly striking, but they possess an elegance of form and colour which can compete with the exotic types of orchids.

Two quite abundant European orchids are the lady's slipper and the vanilla orchid which both grow on the mountains of southern Europe. There are some 125 species of orchid in Europe, including about fifty in Britain, such as man orchids, helleborines, fen orchids and bee, spider and fly orchids.

Whilst the orchids of the tropical forests are all epiphyte or semi-epiphyte (that is they grow between the crevices of the trees but do not live a parasitic existence) the European orchids are ground plants, that is they sink their roots directly into the ground. They all have a small corolla, often grow in clusters and are sometimes delicately scented.

26

Where you can find the most important atomic centres in Europe

An important world record in the field of nuclear science is held by Britain, where the world's first atomic power station was built in 1956 at Calder Hall.

With its production of 180 megawatts of electricity, the plant at Calder Hall was outclassed by the one built in 1971 at Wylfa Point, in Anglesey, which produces 1,180 megawatts of electricity, one thousand more than its forerunner. Further plants with a capacity of 1,320 megawatts are being built at Hinkley Point, Hartlepool and Heysham.

Of all European countries, Great Britain probably still possesses the largest number of nuclear centres which produce atomic energy for peaceful needs. Various types of reactors are used in these centres. Noteworthy are: the B central at Dungeness which is one of the more advanced gas reactors (AGR), the heavy water reactor at Winfrith, and the fast-breeder reactor at Dounreay.

France, too, possesses nuclear reactors of notable size: in particular there are the Rhapsodie, built in collaboration with Euratom, and the four nuclear centres on the Loire, at Chinon. Germany, Italy and the eastern European countries also have very efficient nuclear centres.

Nuclear reactors are being rapidly improved and they offer us, for the future, an abundant supply of nuclear energy destined to replace what today we get mainly from traditional sources: carbon, petrol and hydro-electric energy.

Meanwhile, scientists are busy studying the possibility of building a plant which will reproduce the same energy as that generated by the stars.

Where you can still find seals in the Mediterranean

Along the rocky, uninhabited coasts of Sardinia lives an animal whose habits are still largely unknown: the monk seal. This seal, which comes from the same family as the polar seal, lives in the depths of sub-marine caves and is the only pinniped, or fin-footed animal, acclimatized to the Mediterranean. It feeds on fish and molluscs.

It is forbidden by law to hunt these animals and yet their survival is due more to their natural prudence which makes them instinctively seek refuge in deep holes which are reached through the mouths of the sub-marine caves.

An excellent swimmer, like all other seals, the monk seal lives principally in water and can remain totally immersed for long periods without breathing.

Calder Hall in Britain; the world's first nuclear power station

Finnish draught horse

Where you can find the land of lakes

Looking at a map, Finland seems like a piece of lace, a tunnel riddled with an infinite number of very characteristic lakes.

Finland has, quite rightly, been called the land of lakes: in fact, from the smallest, which is virtually a puddle, to the largest, the Saimaa situated in the south, it has tens of thousands of lakes which cover 9·4 per cent of the country. This lake district with its inland archipelagos has been less effected by outside influences than the coastal regions.

Someone once said that there are two dominant colours in Finland, blue and green; the blue of the lakes and the green of the forests. If we add to these colours the white of the snow that for a good part of the year covers Finnish territory, we have named the three national colours of Finland. The snow feeds innumerable rivers which often link the lakes.

One feature which may seem strange in country as flat as that in southern Finland is the way the lakes are on different levels. Sometimes characteristic waterfalls, which the Finns have used for the production of electric energy, are formed by a river flowing rapidly from one lake to another.

Where you can find the famous valley of the roses

'The valley of the roses' could be the title of a novel or a romantic film, one of many fantasies; instead it actually exists in Bulgaria.

It is a narrow valley (enclosed by two mountain chains and crossed by the Tundza, the principal tributary of the river Maritza) which at harvest time becomes a sea of roses, a unique spectacle. Until the height of summer every morning at the first signs of dawn the petal pickers fill their large sacks and hurry to deliver their product to be processed before the petals lose their fragrance.

Rose essence, known and appreciated in all parts of the world, is extracted from the petals.

Where there exist many relics of ancient Roman life

Some Roman buildings have come down to us in good condition but these are usually the grand and monumental. We would have little idea of the appearance of a Roman town and its populated districts if Vesuvius had not erupted in A.D. 79. It buried under its ashes two flourishing cities situated in the region of Campania, Pompeii and Herculaneum, which excavation has restored to us almost intact.

Both of these towns were overwhelmed in the middle of their busy lives and it is this daily life that we can see around us as we tour the ancient streets. We admire the Forum with its public buildings, the theatres, the amphitheatre, the gymnasium, the baths and especially the houses with their elegant arcades, painted walls and mosaic floors. There are shops too, such as a type of coffee house where money to pay the last bill had been left on the counter by a customer, or the clothes shop where the owner had painted on his windowsill the emblem of his trade and of his goddess protectress.

Wandering around the dead town, along the streets marked with deep tracks cut by the carts, we can read the electoral notices with which a candidate nearly 2,000 years ago exhorted electors to vote for him.

Where you can find the island of fire

One of the most active volcanic areas in the world is Iceland: in addition to craters which have been dormant since time immemorial, the island has some thirty active volcanoes.

Iceland possesses other volcanic features, such as thermal springs and solfatara (which emit sulphur and water vapour gases); the most notable are the geysers which are jets of water at a high temperature.

The Icelanders have taken advantage of these hot springs: they have directed them into a system of pipes which heat homes, swimming pools and greenhouses. Since 1943 the whole city of Reykjavik has thus been able to solve its heating problems.

Reconstruction of a typical house in Pompeii

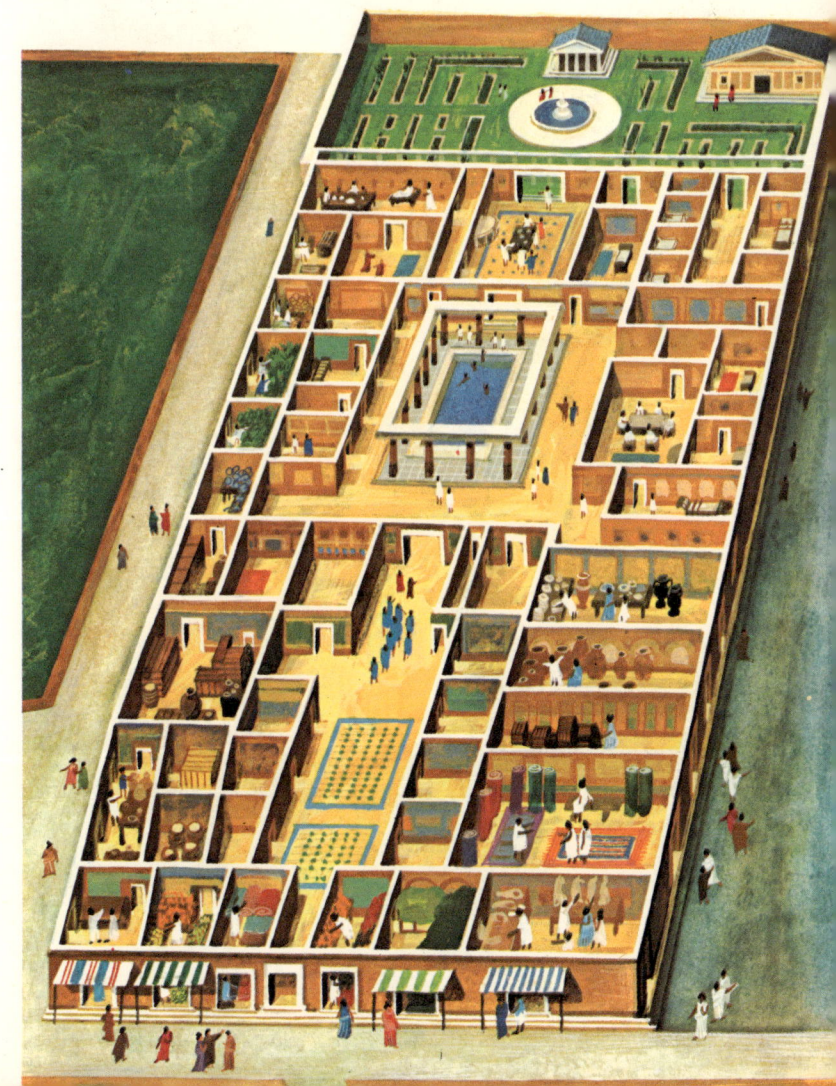

Where the wild cat still lives in Europe

The wild cat is a ferocious, feline animal belonging to the same family as the tiger, the panther and the jaguar. Its size and appearance are the same as those of a large domestic cat, but its fierce temperament and exceptional strength are obvious when it is attacking other creatures.

It can hold its own against three or four dogs and will not hesitate to assault a human being. By day, it lives hidden in holes or in the trees and it goes hunting at night, destroying birds, hares and squirrels.

You would think that such a ferocious beast would live only in distant, primitive regions. It once ranged over Great Britain and central and southern Europe and can still be found in remote parts of Scotland and in all the forests of central Europe, although it is now becoming rather rare.

Where you can find a town made of salt

Beneath the city of Wieliczka in Poland lies one of the most extraordinary sights in the world: a subterranean town made of salt.

This town is in the heart of a salt mine which goes down to over 300 metres below ground and has more than 112 kilometres of tunnels. All the elements that make up the town are built from salt, that is from sodium chloride in a crystalline state, which has a consistency similar to that of porous stone. Everything is made of rock-salt, from the pillars to the lamp-posts, from the streets to the bridges.

There is everything here that you would find in any small town: a church decorated with bas-reliefs, a railway station, a throne-room, a ballroom, small lakes, wide spacious streets. All that is admired in this town is the work of the miners who through decades of patient labour succeeded in completing this colossal task.

Although there are other towns made of salt in both Poland and Austria, Wieliczka is the most complete and most perfect of them all. The salt mines there have been worked for over nine centuries.

Felis sylvestris, a wild cat of Europe

Where fox hunting is a national sport

The home of fox hunting is England. Modern fox hunting developed in the nineteenth century and became a national sport.

Huntsmen usually wear scarlet coats, white cravats and black velvet caps, but in some ancestral hunts run by noble families, green, yellow or grey may be worn instead of scarlet.

To take part in a hunt a good horse which is already familiar with the sport is indispensable. The horse must be able to jump all obstacles from ditches to fences, from metal barriers to blackberry bushes. The rider, too, must be perfect if he does not want to become unsaddled at the first jump.

Besides the horses, it is essential to have a good pack of hounds trained to obey the huntsman's voice and horn by which he controls the hunt. Each pack of hounds has a master who is in charge of the hunt.

Hippocrates and his disciples

Where you can find invaluable remains of Greek civilization

In ancient times towns were built at the foot of fortified elevations which served as strongholds, that is the last area of defence in case of enemy attack. That is why Athens chose the Acropolis, the summit (*acrón*) of the town, as the sight of her 'citadel'.

It is here that the most important buildings were erected and these remain today to testify for one of the most supreme civilizations of all time.

Greek philosophy has remained famous for its original and bold conceptions and Hellenic art has been and still is a source of inspiration to innumerable artists.

The Acropolis of Athens is the epitome of Greek architecture and sculpture. Dominating the whole hill are the ruins of the Parthenon, the temple to Athene conceived by the greatest architects and sculptors of the epoch. Work began on it in 447 B.C. and the building was completed by 438 B.C., although the carvings and decoration were not finished for another six years.

THE WHERE OF AFRICA

Where the water in oases of the Sahara desert comes from

Desert oases occur at points where a spring of water rises to the surface. But where does this water come from, since it hardly ever rains in the desert? To find out we must understand something known as ground water which lies under the soil to form a layer called an aquifer.

In rainy places three things happen to rainfall once it has reached the ground: the rain is carried away in rivers or stored in lakes, it is turned into clouds through evaporation by the heat of the sun, or it seeps through into the soil.

Water seeps through the soil and passes through permeable or porous rocks. When the rainwater meets an impermeable or non-porous rock such as clay or shale, it can go no farther. The rainwater then spreads out to form the aquifer. It lies there like an underground reservoir until it finds an outlet. This occurs when the clay or shale formations break through to the surface. The rainwater then emerges as a spring.

Sometimes these springs are situated far from where the rain first seeped into the soil. This explains why water can be found in arid zones such as deserts.

In the Sahara the spring waters which form the oases have come many hundreds of miles from mountain regions in the north where the rain first fell.

Where the desert rat lives

Desert rats can be seen during moonlit nights scampering and hopping about the desert sands. These animals, also known as jerboas, come out of their hiding places only after dark in search of food.

But they do not seem to be looking for food as they jump about. Their bodies are about 20 centimetres long and the tail, which ends in a tuft, is some 25 centimetres. The front limbs are extremely short while the hind pair are about six times as long. They are very funny to watch as they hop about on their long hind legs that look like those of kangaroos.

Desert rats live in burrows which they dig with their nails and teeth. They are shy animals and this, together with their agility, makes them difficult to catch. They live quite well in captivity, however, and are extremely clean in their habits. They have a sand-coloured coat, as most desert-dwelling animals have.

Where the cheetah hunts its prey

The cheetah is a member of the cat family which lives in the vast stretches of the African savanna where it reigns supreme among animals.

The cheetah is about the same size as a leopard, but its body is much more slender. It has long legs with powerful bared claws, for, unlike other cats, it has no sheaths for retracting its claws. Its coat is of crisp, coarse, sandy-yellow fur with black spots. It is a fierce animal but it will never attack people. In fact, if it is captured while still a cub, it can be domesticated and even kept as a pet. It is not bred in captivity.

The cheetah is one of the swiftest land animals and can reach speeds of between 104 and 112 kilometres an hour. It hunts alone or in small groups, stalking its prey, usually antelopes, and then running it down. Speedy as it is, the antelope cannot escape.

Antelopes are a large group of grass-eating animals who live in the savanna where they can find plenty of food. They vary in size, in the shape of their horns and in the colour of their coats. One of the smallest of the antelope family is the dik-dik which stands only about 30 centimetres high at the shoulders. Like other members of the antelope family the dik-dik lives in large herds.

When antelopes are not feeding they trot along in single file following the oldest male who acts as leader. Their ears and nostrils are always straining for the slightest sound of danger because they know that their chances of escape will be much greater the sooner they find out there is an enemy near.

Where savanna plant life grows

The African savanna is a grassy plain scattered with trees and occurs in places that have warm, dry weather for long periods interrupted by brief spells of heavy rainfall.

During the rainy season the savanna is a brilliant green with tall grass and flowers, but it becomes parched and brown during the dry season. There are few large trees although some of them, like the baobab, have enormous, barrel-like trunks. Much of the savanna's tree life forms part of scrubland which also includes bushes and thorny shrubs.

Where to find dome-shaped huts

There is no other part of the world that has such a wide variety of dwellings as Africa. These homes range from the most primitive huts to modern skyscrapers of advanced design. This is one of the features of Africa today, that it is a land of rich contrasts.

The primitive dwellings of Africa are mainly huts. The word 'hut' to a European has a simple meaning. But in Africa a hut can be a single wall providing shelter from the wind or it can be quite a complicated structure with several floors and built partly with hard materials such as dried clay.

The dome-shaped hut is a typical African home. Sometimes the dome is rather pointed and the hut has an oval shape, resembling a beehive. Dome-shaped huts look like the igloos in which Eskimos live.

Most African huts are simple to build. The men of the village make a framework of intertwined branches which the women then cover with straw, leaves or grass. The roof framework is sometimes built on the ground and then lifted into place, so that it can be easily moved to other walls when the first ones rot. One African tribe called the Benné covers the framework of branches with clay. In Cameroon huts are also covered in clay but the huts have a pointed top. These dome-shaped huts can be quite small, like those built by the pygmies, or they can be as large as a king's palace, as in Uganda. These large huts are more than 8 metres high and 10 metres wide.

The cattle-raising Hottentots who move from one water hole to another, make an easily transported hut of reed mats sewn over a frame of light poles.

Other African peoples who live in huts include the Bushmen of southern Africa, certain Nilotic peoples in north-eastern Africa, the Bantu of southern Africa and some of the Zulu tribes in south-eastern Africa.

Where great herds of zebu are reared

There is an open plain between Kenya and Tanzania where almost the only form of wealth is cattle. This is the land where the Pastoral Masai people live. They have more than a million cattle and cattle-breeding is their main occupation.

Pastoral Masai men and women worry only about their animals. These people still recall a terrible disease that killed many beasts in 1883.

The most commonly raised animal is the zebu, a hump-backed ox. The Pastoral Masai also breed many donkeys, sheep and goats but they have no chickens or other domestic fowl and they do not hunt or grow crops.

Cattle provide the Pastoral Masai with their main foods: milk, meat and blood. Only the women are allowed to milk the cattle. The men take blood from the animals every month by extracting it from the zebu's jugular vein.

The animals are considered so precious that the Pastoral Masai eat meat only on certain feast days. On such days they will not drink milk with their meat. Honey-beer is drunk and most adults chew tobacco or use snuff.

As well as obtaining milk from the zebu, the people like to shape the animals' horns by bending them into various shapes as soon as they start growing.

The Pastoral Masai live in a kraal camp. This consists of a large circular thornbush fence inside which the women build igloo-like mud huts. At night the cattle are taken into the camp as protection against wild animals.

Where to find wild peacocks

Wild peacocks live together in large flocks in the forests of central Africa. They scratch about in the ground during the day for seeds to eat and at nightfall they fly up to the trees where they perch and sleep.

Every peacock has several wives known as peahens. The female birds build their nests on the ground and lay from four to six whitish, sometimes spotted eggs. During the mating season the male utters a harsh raucous cry.

Peacocks were first brought to Europe in the days of Alexander the Great. At one time they used to be kept on many farms, but today they are usually found in zoos or public parks.

Peacocks are extremely beautiful birds with their brightly coloured plumage. The male bird makes a magnificent display when it opens up its huge fan-like tail to preen itself. The female is more dully coloured and does not have the large ornamental feathers.

(above) **Peacock**
(below) **Malay Argus Pheasant**

Where the world's largest ape makes its home

The gorilla lives in the dense forests of equatorial Africa. It is the largest and most powerful of the ape family. The gorilla is extremely strong but it is a placid animal, not dangerous to people unless it is unduly disturbed. But other animals are very much afraid of it: few of them will dare to attack a gorilla because they know they would have the worse of the encounter.

A full-grown gorilla stands nearly 2 metres tall, with a massive body and very muscular arms and legs, and can weigh over 200 kilogrammes. Its jaws jut out and it has a broad, flattened nose and huge beetling eyebrows.

There are two main kinds of gorilla: the lowland gorilla that lives in the rain forests of western Africa, has a dark grey coat; the mountain gorilla which lives in the eastern regions of the Congo-Uganda borderland at altitudes of more than 3,000 metres, has black fur. Little is known about the ways of these big apes. This is because gorillas are very shy animals and also because they were first found only during the last century.

Gorillas usually live in groups which include both young and old. They build rough dwellings in trees a few metres above the ground. These dwellings look like platforms made of branches and twigs.

Gorillas do not spend all their lives in the trees. During the day they wander about on the ground looking for food. They feed on leaves, roots and fruit which the forest has in plenty. Gorillas walk in a crouching position, but every so often they stand up straight on their long hind legs.

Where the optical illusion of mirages occurs

Sometimes when the thirsty traveller makes his way through the burning sands of the desert, a lake suddenly appears before him just over on the horizon. The traveller then makes haste to reach this totally unexpected and welcome place of refreshment. Of course, the lake is not really there and what the traveller sees is a mirage.

For a long time people thought mirages were hallucinations, an unreal vision like a dream that some people experience when they are ill. Then it was discovered that mirages also appeared to people who were perfectly well, who were not hungry or thirsty.

It was then learned that mirages are an optical illusion, a trick played by the air.

The temperature of the air we breathe differs according to the altitude. In the desert, air is warmer near the ground, which can be extremely hot on summer days, and grows cooler as it rises upwards. Warm air is denser than cool air and acts as a mirror or a pool of water to reflect objects. These objects are often reflected upside down as trees are in a still pool of water. The warm, dense air also reflects the sky and the shimmering effect on the ground looks like a lake or pool.

Where the ships of ancient Egypt sailed on their voyages of discovery

The ancient Egyptians believed that the river Nile was a kindly god, the father of their homeland. It was only natural, therefore, that they should want to follow the course of this river up to its source.

The first Egyptian expeditions on which we have any reliable information took place in about 3000 B.C. In these expeditions the Egyptians went as far south as Kush in the land of the Nubian peoples. They also explored the desert to the west as far as Libya and sailed along the Libyan coast in their ships.

One very important Egyptian expedition was ordered by Queen Hatshepsut who reigned from about 1503 to 1482 B.C. It was a very daring venture. The queen sent five ships to the coast of 'the land of Punt', which is now called Somalia. Punt was a city built on stilts whose ruler, a peace-loving king, welcomed the Egyptian explorers and gave them many generous gifts. The queen had the happy experience of seeing her ships return to Egypt laden with myrrh, incense and other fragrant and valuable woods. But the most delighted of all must have been the Egyptian army generals when they saw huge animals be-

The warship of Rameses III, with its battering-ram

ing unloaded from the ships. These animals were elephants and it was plain that they would prove very useful in battle against an enemy.

It was not until 600 B.C. that the Egyptians set out on another expedition of such importance. The Greek historian Herodotus relates how the pharaoh Necho II sent a fleet of Phoenician sailors, the finest navigators of those days, to explore the African coastline. The Phoenicians sailed down the Red Sea and went round the entire continent of Africa. They returned to the Mediterranean Sea through the Pillars of Hercules, known today as the Strait of Gibraltar. The voyage took three years and the Phoenician sailors had to stop for long periods on the way to grow wheat and other crops which they needed for food on their great journey.

Where to find Africa's largest national parks

The animals of Africa, many of them belonging to species which are now rare, today live under special protection from the danger of being hunted into extinction.

These animals live in national parks, huge areas reserved for them in central and eastern Africa. By 1970 there were about thirty-five countries with national parks or reserves which have become great tourist attractions. Every year thousands of people come from all over the world to see the giraffes, elephants, lions, gazelles, rhinoceroses, hippopotamuses and countless species of birds and reptiles living in freedom in these reserves.

There are good tracks and smooth roads and visitors can drive for hundreds of kilometres through these national parks. Some of Africa's most important reserves are in Kenya and Tanzania. The Serengeti National Park in northern Tanzania covers an area of 15,000 square kilometres and extends from Lake Victoria to Mount Kilimanjaro. It has the finest collection of plains animals in Africa and is especially famous for its lions.

There is a park with rich animal life and many birds, especially flamingoes, near Lake Manyara. Visitors can drive close up to the animals in their cars and take photographs.

Hunting is totally forbidden in these parks and game wardens and zoologists are constantly trying to increase the number of animals that live there.

Where to find the Victoria Falls

The Zambesi is one of Africa's longest rivers and gives rise to the world-famous Victoria Falls. These falls were named by the British missionary and explorer David Livingstone who became the first European to see them in 1855.

Livingstone was then exploring the upper reaches of the Zambesi, a river which was almost unknown. The Africans knew where to find this mighty course of water which they called 'the smoke that thunders' because of the noise the falls make as they drop over the cliff. But the Africans were afraid of taking Livingstone to the place: they were superstitious and feared they would be punished by the gods whom, they believed, lived inside the falls.

Livingstone succeeded in persuading the Africans to help him and at last he was able to see one of the most impressive sights in the world as the Zambesi plunged 108 metres down a narrow gorge.

Livingstone was able to produce an almost perfect map of the Zambesi's course, showing the exact location of the Victoria Falls. They are situated at the far eastern end of the border that separates Zambia from Rhodesia. It was not until the railway from Bulawayo was opened in September 1905, however, that many people were able to visit the falls.

Where the cola used in making soft drinks comes from

During the nineteenth century the Africans who acted as porters and carried heavy loads for European explorers had a simple cure for the exhaustion of travelling through the forest: they would gather a few cola seeds and chew them during rest halts.

The Africans knew that cola seeds contain a substance that acts as a stimulant on the body. By chewing cola seeds, these Africans were able to walk for hours without feeling tired. Later, scientists discovered that cola seeds contain the drug caffeine.

The tree on which the cola grows is common throughout western Africa. It became the basis of an important industry when cola began to be used as an ingredient in soft drinks. The trees vary in height, from 10 to 15 metres. The fruit of the tree is star-shaped, each point of the star containing a few seeds, known as cola nuts.

The secretary bird

Where to find the bird that snakes fear

Throughout many regions of Africa from the Tropic of Cancer south to the Cape, there lives a large bird that seems to have declared war on all snakes. This is called the secretary bird, a long-legged relation of the hawk family. The bird gets its name from the long feathers that grow from the back of its head. These feathers resemble quills, or old-fashioned pens, and they make the bird look like a clerk with pens stuck behind his ears.

The secretary bird is over a metre tall. It is one of the most powerful birds of prey and has a fierce curved beak. Its favourite food is snakes, including poisonous ones.

There is no bird that can rival the secretary bird for agility. This bird relies on its swiftness to catch and kill snakes while at the same time leaping back to avoid their poisonous bite.

When the secretary bird attacks it holds its short wings forward like a shield. The wings have bony knobs on them which help to protect the bird from bites and are also useful weapons for attacking its prey.

Where the religious festival of Ramadan is celebrated

Fasting is an important part of the religion of Islam practised by Moslems. The fast takes place during a period known as Ramadan. This is a lunar month, or twenty-eight days, before the time of the pilgrimage to Mecca. This month was chosen because it was then that 'the Koran was sent down as a guidance for the people'.

According to the Koran, during Ramadan all Moslems who have reached the age of reason must not eat or drink between dawn and dusk.

African Moslems also practise Ramadan very carefully. In the city of Fez, for example, where there is a famous Arab university, students are excused work during Ramadan so that they can pray and meditate.

In Tunisia Ramadan is observed with great solemnity during the fourteenth and twentieth days. Government ministers take part in the religious ceremonies. The Libyan people also observe the fasting period with great solemnity. In Senegal, in western Africa, there are many practising Moslems. Only special cases are allowed to break the day-long fasts. These include the very young, the old, the sick and people who are travelling.

Ramadan ceremonies are very impressive and sometimes last for several days. They usually take place towards the end of Ramadan to bring this month to a fitting conclusion.

Where to find 'the traveller's tree'

The *ravenala* is a beautiful, decorative plant that grows in Madagascar, which is one of the largest islands in the world. The plant is shaped like a huge fan made of feathers and stands more than 10 metres high.

The large boat-shaped leaves of the *ravenala* resemble those of the banana plant. They fan outwards from a short, smooth trunk made up of the stems of earlier leaves that have died. In old *ravenala* trees this trunk becomes hard and as thick as a man's body.

In the language of Madagascar *ravenala* means 'the traveller's tree'. According to old beliefs this tree produces water at the base of its leaves and thus is valuable to a traveller.

The tree does not really produce water: it is rain which has been trapped in the sheaths that cover the *ravenala*'s leaves. The water can be obtained by pricking the stems of the leaves and has been used for drinking in times of scarcity. The seeds of the *ravenala* contain starch and are eaten by the people of Madagascar, who also boil the young leaves which taste rather like cabbage.

Where Africa's chief Moslem centres are located

The Islamic religion is widespread in Africa, especially in the north. In some countries, such as Mauritania, Libya, Tunisia and Algeria, Islam is the official religion of the state. There are a large number of Moslems in other countries of Africa, especially Egypt, Sudan, Senegal, Morocco, Somalia, Niger and Nigeria.

Mosques are the Moslem places of worship. The most famous include those at Tlemcen and Algiers in Algeria; the Koutoubiya in Marrakesh; the Kairouine at Fez; and the Mansur in Meknes. The great Kairouan mosque in Tunisia is also famous.

Every mosque has one or more minarets. These are tall slender towers from which the muezzin, or priest, calls the people to prayer five times a day. When they hear the wailing of the muezzin, Moslems kneel down and pray, facing towards Mecca.

Where the desert viper lives

There is an incredible number of extremely poisonous vipers in the Sahara desert. They hide by burying themselves in the sand and lie in wait for their prey.

Even while walking very carefully a person can accidentally tread on one of these snakes. The consequences can be very serious.

The most common desert viper is the *cerastes*, also known as the horned viper. This snake has two horn-like growths above its eyes that give it a very fierce look. It is a rare species for most horned vipers have only one horn. This reptile is hunted and sold to zoos because it is so uncommon.

Where the ancient Egyptians obtained papyrus

The paintings in the tombs of the ancient Egyptians contain many illustrations of papyrus rolls and numerous examples of the rolls themselves have been found. The papyrus plant was cultivated along the banks of the river Nile. Today it has almost disappeared from the lower reaches of the river but it still flourishes in the upper Nile regions and in Ethiopia and Syria as well as in parts of southern Europe.

Our word 'paper' comes from 'papyrus'. This is because the ancient Egyptians used papyrus plants to make a material for writing on. Some ancient Egyptian papyrus writings date from 3600 B.C.

Today papyrus is used as an ornamental plant. It grows on marshes or by rivers to a height of more than 5 metres.

Where Stanley and Livingstone met

In 1849 the British missionary and explorer David Livingstone crossed the Kalahari Desert in southern Africa. He reached the river Zambesi which he explored. He later went up the river and discovered the great falls which he named after Queen Victoria. From 1858 to 1864, Livingstone explored the headwaters of the river Congo, of Lake Nyasa, Benguelo, Mweru, Tanganyika and the river Luluaba. He was recalled to England in 1864, but after a year he returned to Africa. When no news at all was received in Britain of Livingstone's whereabouts, many people feared he was dead. An expedition was organized to go out in search of the missionary. Henry Stanley, a British-born journalist working for an American newspaper, led the expedition.

Stanley finally found Livingstone in 1871 at Ujiji on the eastern shore of Lake Tanganyika. The meeting between the two men seemed very casual, as if they had bumped into each other in a London street. When Stanley saw Livingstone after searching the dark continent for him, he greeted him simply with: 'Dr Livingstone, I presume'.

Livingstone died in 1873 of tropical fever. Stanley went back to Africa several times and his name is now associated with the exploration of the Congo river basin and with the finding of the governor of the Equatorial province of Egypt, Emin Pasha, who had been abandoned by rebels in the heart of Africa.

Stanley was a fine writer and wrote many exciting books about his African journeys. He died in London in 1904.

Livingstone aroused British conscience about the African question

Stanley found Livingstone at Ujiji

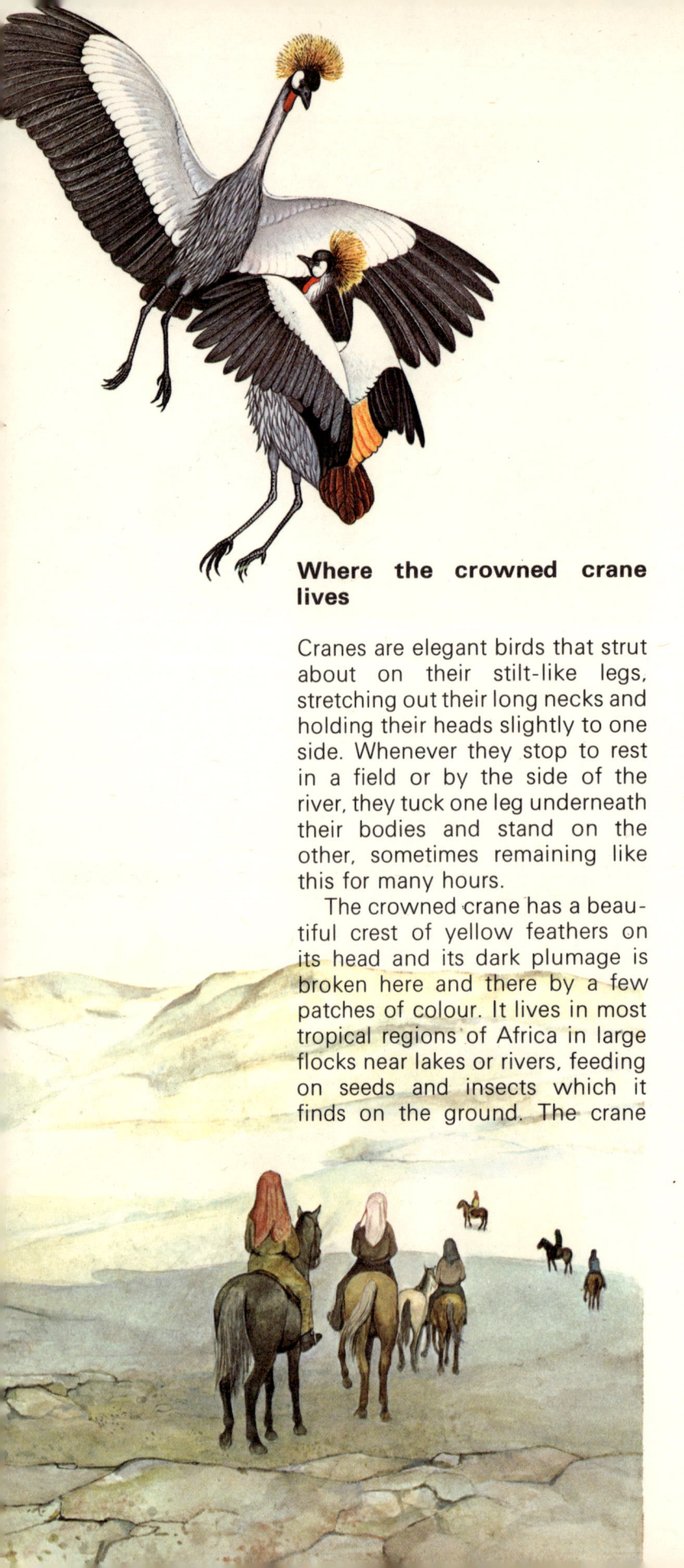

flies up to the trees after dark to spend the night safely perched on a branch.

Where the nomads of northern Africa roam

In parts of the Spanish Sahara, there are many people who live a nomadic, or wandering, life. These nomads are shepherds and live in black goat-hair tents, where they shelter from the burning rays of the sun as their flocks graze and search for food which is none too plentiful.

The Berbers of Algeria who used to be farmers, became nomads to avoid the unending invasions of their fertile but unsafe valleys. To escape from their enemies, they took to the mountains of the Atlas range and to the high plateau of the Sahara desert where they became nomads and raised livestock. What they did was unusual because more often nomads become settled farmers and few tribes change to a wandering life.

In Libya, many nomad tribes live near places where engineers drill for oil. The nomad's life is very hard: there is the great heat of the burning desert sands and winds that can sometimes blow at more than 100 kilometres an hour.

The nomads of Libya are also known as the Tuareg. When they move from place to place they travel on camels, without which it would be impossible to make long journeys across the desert.

Nomad tribes also live in the Sudan where they form about 14 per cent of the population. They breed livestock and are always looking for supplies of water and grazing grounds for their animals.

Where the crowned crane lives

Cranes are elegant birds that strut about on their stilt-like legs, stretching out their long necks and holding their heads slightly to one side. Whenever they stop to rest in a field or by the side of the river, they tuck one leg underneath their bodies and stand on the other, sometimes remaining like this for many hours.

The crowned crane has a beautiful crest of yellow feathers on its head and its dark plumage is broken here and there by a few patches of colour. It lives in most tropical regions of Africa in large flocks near lakes or rivers, feeding on seeds and insects which it finds on the ground. The crane

Goulimine

Man in djellaba

Woman in haik

Berber

Where the salt road passes through the Sahara

In addition to water, camels and mutton, salt is a valuable commodity for barter among the Tuareg desert nomads who find plentiful supplies of it in the Hoggar, a mountain range in the central Sahara.

When the rainy season is over at the end of June, the 'salt caravan' sets out from the Hoggar. For the Tuareg people this is a very important event.

For weeks the workers in every encampment have filled up sacks with salt. When the time comes to set out only those people who cannot face the rigours of the desert stay behind: women, children and old people. The most experienced of the Tuareg is the camel leader and behind him all the camels are linked together in a long line. The Tuareg stop along the way at oases where they leave supplies of food to eat on the return journey. When the rainy season starts, the Tuareg caravan stops at the edge of the desert so that the rain will not spoil their goods. By the end of October the Tuareg reach their destination which is Niger or Chad. The return journey takes three months and the caravan, consisting of between 100 and 150 camels, is laden with goods obtained through barter: millet, rugs, sugar and various cloths.

The rocks that line the caravan trail are marked with scratches, some a few days old and others thousands of years. This is *tifinagh*, the mysterious hand-writing which the Tuareg have used since they began their wanderings 4,000 years ago.

A swamp with mangrove trees

Where trees defy the sea

In the river estuaries of tropical Africa, dense thickets or forests of mangroves push their many roots into the mud of the river bank and prevent it from being washed away. These trees make it possible for a forest to grow right up to the sea.

Mangroves belong to many plant families, all of which send out their roots through the air from their trunks and branches. There are so many of these roots that they form a massive tangle that no one can penetrate.

Mangroves look especially impressive at low tide when their innumerable curling roots emerge from the mud. They have evergreen leaves and produce thin fruits which are about 90 centimetres long.

Where raffia comes from

Raffia is a plant fibre that can be woven. It is obtained from the young leaves of a palm that grows in the marshy regions of Madagascar.

This palm does not produce edible fruit, but it is extremely useful because of its fibre. It also produces wax and a beverage known as palm wine. The raffia palm is from 5 to 10 metres high and has about twenty leaves that form a tuft at the top of the sturdy trunk.

The leaves are about 2 metres long. They are cut from the plant before they begin to curl. The underside is removed in strips which are dried in the sun. They then go through certain processes to make them into the shape and colour found in shops.

The wax is obtained from the surface of the leaves and looks like a sticky powder. This is dissolved and then pressed into cakes and used in certain industries.

The sap of the raffia palm also provides a delicious drink.

Where the Nile rises

The nineteenth century was the age of great explorations of Africa when, one by one, the secrets of the dark continent were revealed. One of the mysteries that drove so many explorers to Africa was that which surrounded the source of the river Nile, probably the longest river in the world, that flows for 6,690 kilometres through forests and deserts.

It was John Speke, a British explorer, who discovered the sources of the Nile. Speke was born in 1827 and served in the Indian army. He was thirty when he made his great discovery.

Speke set out from Zanzibar accompanied by Richard Burton. The two men headed for central Africa by way of Lake Tanganyika. A few months later, in 1859, Speke arrived alone at a great lake which he named Victoria in honour of the British monarch. Speke had the feeling that the Nile began somewhere in that region. In 1862 he travelled along the west bank of Lake Victoria together with his fellow-countryman James Grant and discovered a river, the turbulent waters of which rushed into the lake. For Speke there were no more doubts: from that river, named the Kagera, came the waters which first formed the lake and then the Nile. Speke telegraphed London that the source of the Nile had been found. He was right and the great mystery had been solved.

Where Africa's chief mineral deposits lie

Africa is often called 'the land of the future' because of its great natural resources. It has a total land area of 30,300,000 square kilometres and some 352,841,000 inhabitants (eleven persons to the square kilometre). Europe, by contrast, is one-third the size of Africa and has twice the population. Also many of the people of Africa still live in backward conditions in terms of technical and scientific progress, and as a result a large part of Africa is still undeveloped.

It would not be enough for African progress if the continent had more people but no mineral resources. Africa, however, does have rich natural resources.

Let us quote a few examples. The Sahara is enormously rich in petroleum. These oil deposits have only just begun to be tapped and the reserves appear to be immeasurably vast. Libya is today the world's sixth-greatest producer of petroleum. Its production of crude oil grew from nothing in 1960 to 90 million tons in 1967.

Of course petrol could be challenged in the distant future by another source of power: uranium. Africa has excellent deposits of this mineral. Some are in Katanga, in Zaire, the state that used to be called Congo. Katanga is believed to be one of the world's richest mineral zones. As well as uranium and cobalt, which are radioactive minerals, Katanga also has copper, gold, tin, manganese and cadmium. Zaire is the world's biggest producer of diamonds.

Another country with a rich store of valuable minerals is South Africa. This country produces more than one half of the world's gold in the Transvaal region. The country also has large deposits of diamonds, iron, copper, tin, lead, nickel and coal. The South Africans also extract uranium from the mineral that produces gold. But there is an unhappy side to all this wealth. Most of the riches go to the white people: the blacks, who form two-thirds of the population of South Africa, receive only a few crumbs.

Rhodesia also has important mineral deposits: the main ones are coal, iron and gold.

All these minerals we have mentioned are only a very small part of Africa's natural wealth. Still more treasure lies buried in the earth waiting to be discovered.

Where the desert nomads pitch their tents

The desert nomad's tent is light and easy to erect or dismantle. When the caravan of people and animals halts on its travels, the nomads choose a sheltered spot behind the sand dunes, away from the desert wind.

The women pitch the tents. They begin by digging deep holes in the ground and into these they put poles which form the basic framework of the tents.

The tent walls are made of matting which the nomads buy from the negro markets in Niger. There are no proper doors to the tent: the nomads roll up the matting and enter their home from whatever side they like.

The roof of the tent is put on last. It is made of goat or camel hair which the women weave into material on simple looms.

The nomad's broad and low tent is anchored to the ground by strong ropes. The tent is not a rigid structure and can therefore endure the raging winds and sandstorms of the Sahara.

Where the pygmies live

The broad band of dense forests that cover the equatorial zone of Africa are scattered here and there by clearings where small tribes of pygmies live. The pygmies are the smallest people in the world and are descended from an ancient race that once inhabited Africa. Today the pygmies live much as they have always done for thousands of years and still have very primitive conditions. They are afraid of the white man and try to remain isolated from the rest of the world. Occasionally they visit Bantu villages on the edge of the forests to trade the animals they have caught for tools and arrowheads.

Many scientists believe the pygmies are descended from an ancient human stock that was once widespread throughout Africa. Pygmies are now confined to the forests but there is proof that at one time they lived over a wider region. For example, Homer once described the terrifying battle between dwarf men and cranes, and Herodotus said the pygmies lived in the Libyan desert and were driven south by other invading peoples. Aristotle, too, referred to pygmies as inhabitants of the marshy regions round the source of the river Nile.

There were pygmies at the court of the pharaohs of Egypt where they proved to be skilful dancers and jugglers. Egyptian records show that 4,500 years ago pygmies were inhabiting some of the areas they still occupy today.

Apart from these early accounts, little is known about the origin of these people who are now reduced to living in very difficult conditions in the forests.

Where termites are found

Termites cause severe damage to wooden structures and products, especially in the tropics. They are pale, soft-bodied insects which live in large colonies, feeding mainly on dead grass, leaves and wood, although some eat fungi.

Their ability to build or to destroy is enormous: in a few hours they can destroy an entire wooden hut and they can also build termite hills more than 10 metres high and 20 metres wide.

Termites live mostly in the savanna lands in America, Australia and Africa. They love a warm, dry climate. The ideal temperature for them is between 16° and 26° Centigrade. Termite hills are a perfect refuge against enemies and are cool inside when the weather outside is blazing hot.

The African savanna land, such as that around Accra in Ghana, is marked here and there by these enormous structures which give the surrounding landscape a rather lunar appearance. The largest are called 'termite cities' because they look like a group of miniature skyscrapers.

Two kinds of soldier termites

Hausa baskets

Where the Hausa live

The Hausa are a people who make up about a third of the total population of northern Nigeria and total some 6 million. Some of them are fine-boned and resemble the Tuareg tribesmen who live in the desert; others are powerfully built, dark-skinned and look more like negroes.

The early Hausa were pagans but Islam was introduced at the end of the fourteenth century and gradually spread among the people. A small number of pagan Hausa still exist today in some rural districts.

The Hausa have always had a highly developed talent for trade. For this reason traces of them can be found all over northern and central Africa.

The most important Hausa zones are Kano, Sokoto and Bauchi in Nigeria. As early as the sixteenth century the cities of Katsina and Kano were flourishing centres of trade and Moslem culture.

The Hausa specialize in the trade of arts and crafts at which they are very skilful. These include dyed goods, pottery, cloth, wrought iron, clothes, embroidery and carvings. These Hausa products show a high degree of development.

Where the Kei apple grows

The *Aberia* or Kei apple tree derives its name from Mount Aber in Ethiopia where the first tree of this species was found in that county. The Kei apple, however, grows in its natural state only in southern Africa, in the Cape of Good Hope and Natal, where it grows wild in the Kei Valley.

The trees of the *Aberia* family are shrubby and thorny and can grow to a height of 10 metres. The leaves alternate with rather small flowers. The Kei apple tree is very thorny and in southern Africa it is used as a hedge or a fence.

The common name of the velvety, bright yellow fruit is due to its resemblance to an apple although it is only between 2 and 4 centimetres in diameter and is more the size of a plum. The fruit is very popular in the regions where it grows and is eaten fresh. It has a sugary flesh with a slightly sour tang. The fruit has a pleasant smell and its flavour improves when it is cooked. Kei apples are good for making jam and jelly and attempts are being made to grow the plant in other tropical regions for industrial purposes.

Where the world's largest tree grows

The baobab is a fairly common tree in the dry regions of central Africa and especially in the savanna. It is a very strange tree and typical of these regions. It is not very tall, growing only to a height of some 20 metres, but its trunk is enormous and in some cases reaches 9 metres in diameter.

The baobab rises out of the ground like some huge gasometer. A few short branches grow out from the trunk and the tree has such a strange appearance that an old Arabian legend declares that 'the devil plucked up the baobab, thrust its branches into the earth, and left its roots in the air'.

The inside of the trunk is designed to withstand conditions of long drought: the wood is soft and spongy, full of small holes filled with water obtained during the rainy season and stored there for use during the dry season.

For this reason the wood of the baobab tree is not very good for building or making furniture, although sometimes the trunks of living trees are hollowed out to form houses. The tree's bark is made of a very tough fibre used in making rope and coarse woven materials.

Where the okapi lives

The okapi is an animal that remained completely unknown until 1900. It lives only in the dense jungles of the Congo and is very difficult to find.

The okapi's hindquarters and legs are covered in black and white stripes, in strong contrast to the rest of the animal's body which is reddish-brown in colour. These black and white stripes immediately identify the okapi. On closer examination this grass-eating animal reveals several other individual characteristics.

The okapi resembles but is smaller than the giraffe, with shorter legs and neck. It has large ears and, like the giraffe, the male okapi has a pair of short horns covered in fur except at the tips. The okapi feeds on leaves and shoots which it bites away from the branches of trees.

Unlike the giraffe which lives in the savanna, the okapi prefers the dense forest where this timid animal can hide itself easily. It is a shy, nocturnal animal that lives singly or in pairs.

Where the Masai live

The Masai are a people who live in the steppes of eastern Africa, broad, open plains. Some 50,000 live in Tanzania and 154,000 in Kenya.

The Masai are divided into five districts: Kaputi, Enaiposa, Laikipia, Uasin-gisa and Kisongo. There are four tribes: Aizer, Mengana, Mokezen and Molelyan. The Aizer provide the political and religious leader of all the Masai, known as *doiboni*. This man must be able to see into the future and have magical powers.

The Kwavi, a settled people, are also part of the Masai. Other members are the N'dorobo, who live by hunting and gathering wild food, and the Datoga.

Where to find negroes who have never been influenced by white people

Darfur is the westernmost province of the Sudan. It includes the mountainous region of Jabal Marra which rises to a height of 3,088 metres. Amid the rugged peaks of these mountains live a negro people who, cut off from modern civilization, have retained all their ancient ways of life.

The Fur represent the most northerly negro inhabitants in Africa. Their territory is surrounded by lands inhabited by Berbers and people of Arab origin who have lighter skins. But the Fur have never been influenced by their neighbours.

The region where the Fur live is still little known. Its mountains have made it a safe refuge for hundreds of years and the Fur people have worked as farmers and livestock breeders undisturbed during all that time.

The mountains of Darfur were formed from the molten lava of volcanoes. The soil is very fertile and there is plenty of water. In the sunny valleys farmers grow lemons and mandarin oranges. On the upper slopes, millet, sorghum, wheat and other cereal crops are cultivated by primitive methods.

The most important work of the Fur concerns their animals. During the summer these animals are taken to pastures high up on the mountains. During the rest of the year the herds are kept near the villages. The Fur who live lower down in the valleys keep many camels. Those who live higher up in the mountains keep cattle to obtain milk and meat.

An odd feature of the Fur is the fact that the women work in the fields and the men look after the animals.

The development of the Fur has been held back by lack of communications. In March 1959 the railway was extended to Nyala and this makes it easier to communicate with the outside world.

Where the great civilizations of Africa flourished

The first picture that emerges from the ancient history of Africa is the Egypt of the pharaohs with its temples and colossal tombs.

Egyptian civilization was one

Bearded mask from the Ivory Coast

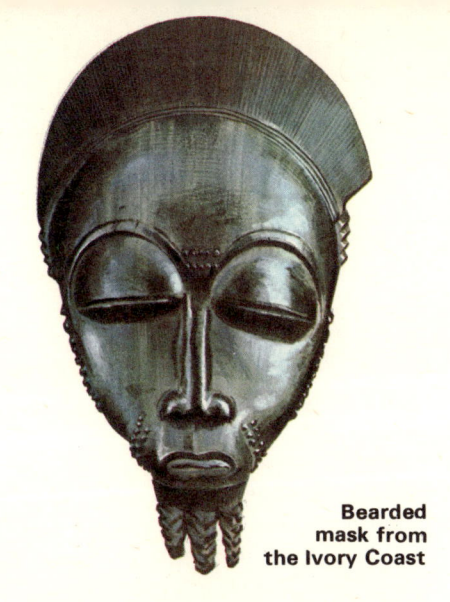

of the highest points of development reached by man. But there were other civilizations in Africa which produced cultures that had far-reaching effects. These other civilizations are being discovered today and their importance to man is being evaluated.

The Carthaginian civilization on the Mediterranean coast of Africa was one of these. It was founded by Phoenician merchants who used Carthage as a base for their daring sea journeys. Carthage became a great naval power and strong enough to challenge the might of ancient Rome.

There were other civilizations outside the Mediterranean region. A Dutch traveller in 1602 described the city of Benin on the western coast of the continent. Benin was the capital of a great kingdom that stood where Nigeria is today. The Dutch traveller wrote of the city's paved roads, its tall defensive towers and the deep moat, the well-planned houses and the magnificent royal palace with its many rooms and chambers.

Before the great days of Benin, about the tenth century A.D., the great empire of Ghana reached its peak. The people of this empire travelled through the sandy wastes of the Sahara to trade between the north of the continent and the so-called 'black Africa' in the south. The trade was in salt, gold, ivory and slaves and covered a territory almost as vast as Europe.

Around the eastern coast of Africa there flourished for several hundred years the kingdom of Monomotapa. The wealth of this kingdom came from mines which provided gold, copper, iron and tin. Explorers have found between the rivers Zambesi and Limpopo the imposing ruins of this civilization. In this region farming was so advanced that crops were grown on huge terraces built on the mountain sides. These farmlands were irrigated by man-made canals and had smooth roads.

Perhaps the oldest empire of central Africa was Ethiopia which flourished 1,000 years before the birth of Christ. This empire has remained intact to our own day, despite endless Islamic invasions. The Ethiopians are a proud people who believe they are descended from the tribe that was once ruled by King David and King Solomon.

Bronze figures from precolonial Nigeria

53

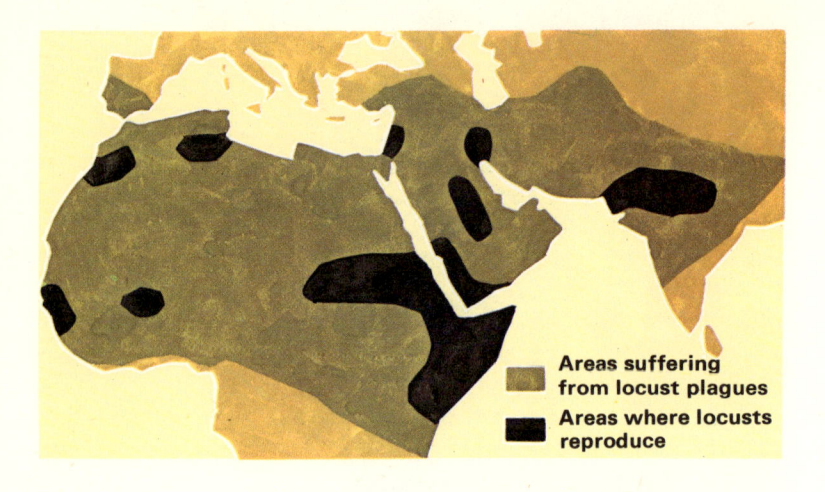

Where the most terrible of the locust plagues take place

It seems incredible that such a harmless-looking insect as the locust has been able to cause the deaths of hundreds of thousands of human beings. Yet in 1867, for example, locusts invaded Algeria and devoured every form of vegetation. The result was a famine in which half a million people died.

(above) A swarm of locusts
An aeroplane spraying insecticide

The fatal danger presented by the locust is its insatiable hunger. When these insects are in small numbers they do no great damage. But when they fly in dark clouds of millions and millions that blot out the light of the sun, they swoop down to earth and devour every scrap of green in minutes.

One of the worst-hit zones is the Mediterranean coast of Africa. The Bible speaks of the terrible plague of locusts that attacked ancient Egypt. Other regions in the north and in the middle of Africa have also suffered greatly. In Algeria, in 1890 and 1891, emergency measures were taken against these dreaded insects. The operations were quite successful: some 95,550 double decalitres of locust eggs were destroyed together with 8,611,336 double decalitres of instars, the little grubs that grow up into locusts.

Today the war on locusts is waged with powerful weapons. These include deadly insecticides sprayed from aeroplanes over the breeding grounds of the locust and at swarms of locust in flight.

Where geraniums first came from

The geraniums we know first came from southern Africa but they are not true geraniums and belong to a plant family known as *Pelargonium*.

There are two main varieties of the plant which people commonly call geranium. The most common has a straight stem; the other variety is climbing or trailing. True geraniums are wild flowers that grow in meadows and forest clearings often high up in mountains. These flowers include the crane's-bills and herb Roberts.

Where man's earliest ancestors lived

In recent years archaeologists have found several fossilized skulls of man-like creatures known as hominids. These remains have been found in East Africa and indicate that this might have been the cradle of the human race.

We know that we may all have descended from an ape-like hominid known as *Australopithecus* who lived about 3 million years ago and who walked in an almost erect position. *Australopithecus* was followed by *Homo habilis* who was able to make a few simple tools from stone. Next came *Homo erectus*, meaning 'the man who stands up straight', and from him there developed *Homo sapiens*, a more intelligent development of the human race.

The main difference between these categories was the size of the brain: a capacity of 500 cubic centimetres for *Australopithecus* and of 1,500 for *Homo sapiens*.

But in 1972 the British anthropologist Richard Leakey found a skull in Kenya that belonged to a hominid with a brain capacity of 800 cubic centimetres. Leakey estimated the age of the skull as 2,600,000 years. This meant the owner of the skull lived about a million years before *Homo habilis* and had a bigger brain. Leakey's discovery set off new studies into the origin of man.

Excavation on the site of fossil remains

THE WHERE OF ASIA

Where the evil-smelling *Rafflesia* flourishes

The *Rafflesia* grows in the mountain forests of Malaysia. It is a parasite and grows on large woody vines, the seeds germinating in the rough bark of the stems of the vine which lie on the ground. The *Rafflesia* has no green, for it does not contain chlorophyll, which gives plants their green colour.

The leaves of the *Rafflesia* are like small fish-scales and the only unusual feature of the plant is its flower. This has a fetid smell resembling that of rotting meat, which attracts several kinds of insects.

Rafflesia flowers are usually large. They have five limp, fleshy petal-like segments of a reddish- or purplish-brown colour which grow out of a very short stalk.

The largest *Rafflesia* known is the *Rafflesia arnoldi* which has flowers more than a metre across of a very bright red dotted with white. It is found in the equatorial forests of Sumatra and Java.

Where the raw material for strychnine is produced

Dense forests containing trees and and plant life of many kinds cover much of south-east Asia near the equator, where the climate is hot and moist. In regions where there is less rain, the soil is dry and scorched for most of the year. It is in these places that the *nux vomica* tree grows from which the poison strychnine is obtained.

The *nux vomica* flourishes in India and Indo-China. It is a majestic tree with thick foliage and the trunk can measure 3 to 4 metres in circumference. Its fruits resemble oranges. Buried inside the extremely bitter pulp are from five to eight seeds from which strychnine is extracted.

Where the armies of Alexander the Great marched

Alexander III of Macedonia was a mighty soldier whose ambition was to conquer the entire world and rule it. In the summer of 327 B.C. he led his army on a campaign towards Asia, entering lands that no one had previously dared to visit. He crossed the river Indus, entering the vast territory of India.

Alexander and his soldiers conquered every army that tried to stop them. He finally reached the Thar desert, a huge, unexplored and mysterious place that lay along what is now the border between India and Pakistan. Alexander was only twenty-nine years old and he wanted to march on eastwards on his great road to conquest. But his soldiers were tired and refused to go further in the tropical rain. Alexander agreed to go back and returned to his homeland. Because of his magnificent exploits he became known as Alexander the Great.

Where the 'Roof of the World' is located

The highest mountain in the world is in the Himalayas: it is Mount Everest. For hundreds of years nobody succeeded in reaching the summit. The people of Tibet called it Chomolungma, meaning 'father of mountains', and believed that strange wild creatures wandered about the mountain's perpetual snows.

Many people thought it would be impossible to measure or climb Mount Everest. The British, who ruled India until after the Second World War, established an office in the 1800s to survey the mountain and measure it. The man who had the idea to start the office was George Everest and he also wanted to measure all the other mountains in the Himalayas. After much work the task was completed in 1852. The height was finally calculated as 8,840 metres (later established more precisely as 8,882 metres). The mountain was named after Everest in 1863.

Another century passed before the peak of Everest was finally reached. In 1953 Edmund Hillary, a New Zealander, and Sherpa Tenzing, a skilled mountaineer of Nepal, climbed to the summit. Hillary and Tenzing had to wear oxygen masks to help them breathe in the thin air. The two climbers planted the flags of Britain, Nepal, India and the United Nations on the peak on which man had never before set foot.

Where the elephants of Asia live

The elephants of Asia roam freely in parts of India, Thailand and Sumatra. Some elephants still live in Indo-China but many were destroyed during the fighting and bombing of the Vietnam war.

The elephants we see at circus performances trained to do many tricks come from Asia. Asian elephants are tamer and quieter than the elephants of Africa. The Asian elephant is smaller than the African one: an Asian bull, or male, elephant is about 3 metres tall and weighs between 3 and 6 tons. It also has smaller ears and a hollow forehead.

In Asia many elephants are trained to do heavy work in the forests. The elephants use their long, powerful trunks to lift huge logs of timber or roll them along the ground.

Elephants are fairly long-lived animals. The normal life-span for an Asian elephant living in its natural surroundings is about fifty years, but one captive elephant in India is recorded to have lived to an age of 130 years.

White elephants, also known as albinos, are rare. They occasionally appear in Siam and Burma where they are regarded as sacred and never allowed to work.

Where camphor comes from

Camphor comes from the camphor laurel which grows in Formosa, China and Japan. It is a vegetable oil with an aromatic smell and is found in all parts of the tree. Usually the camphor is obtained from the leaves which are gathered twice a year and chopped up. The camphor oil is then extracted from the leaves and distilled.

In 1909 scientists invented a way to make artificial camphor and about half the camphor used commercially is now produced synthetically.

Where to find the most beautiful city in Japan

The cities of Japan have grown extremely rapidly since the Second World War mainly because of the spread of new industries which provided work for people but made the cities rather ugly. One city escaped this fate: Kyoto, the ancient capital of Japan founded by the Emperor Kwammu in A.D. 794. For a thousand years Kyoto was the capital of the Japanese empire. During this time it became rich in monuments and the architecture of its buildings resembled that of Chinese cities. Kyoto had stout walls built all round it as a defence against attackers and the city was approached through eighteen gates in the walls. Inside were many gardens and temples of the Buddhist and Shinto religions.

Kyoto is also famous for its works of art and craftsmanship, especially porcelain and silks, and is today visited by many tourists.

Where the city of Troy stood

Until the 1850s many historians thought that the great adventures described by Homer in the *Iliad* and *Odyssey* were all fables which had existed only in the poet's imagination. But between 1870 and 1890 excavations carried out by a German businessman, Heinrich Schliemann, established not only that the great city had actually existed but that nine different Troys had stood on the spot. Each city had been destroyed and a new one rebuilt during a period of 3,000 years.

Later excavations by other archaeologists confirmed Schliemann's belief that these ruins were really the remains of Troy. The archaeologists also found that the seventh stratum, or layer, of the ruins dated back to the great battles and siege in which this city, ruled by King Priam, was destroyed. Today we are certain that Troy did exist and that its towers rose from the summit of a hill called Hisarlik that now stands in Turkey by the waters of the Hellespont.

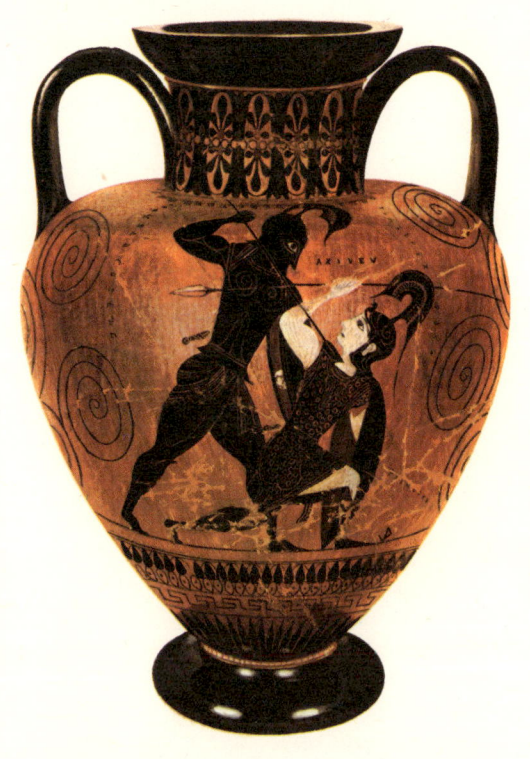

Where the art of *ikebana* and bonsai was born

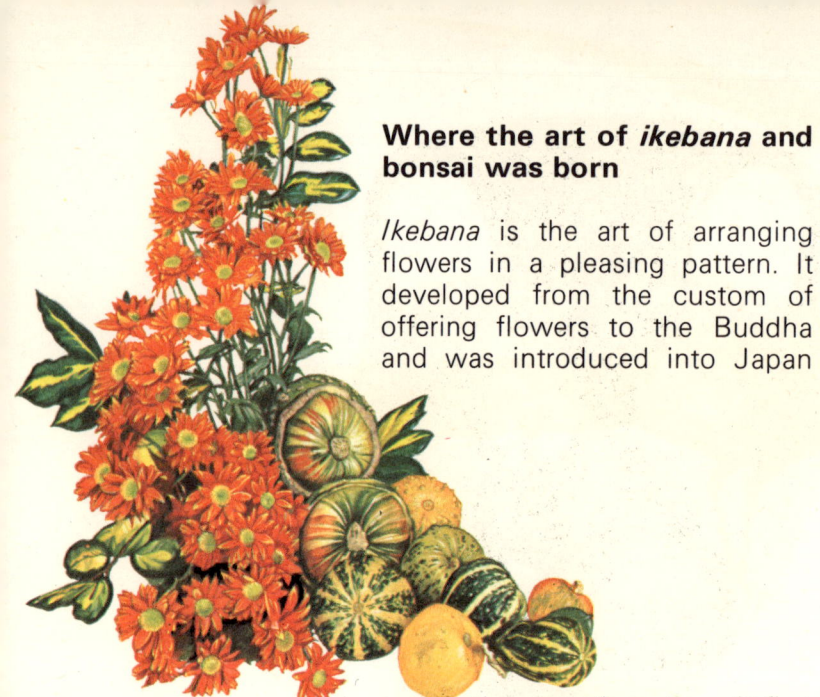

Ikebana is the art of arranging flowers in a pleasing pattern. It developed from the custom of offering flowers to the Buddha and was introduced into Japan early in the seventh century. At first *ikebana* was used only as a form of worship of the Buddha. Priests decorated Buddhist temples with flower arrangements which were not only beautiful but also symbolized various religious ideas. Later, towards the thirteenth century, *ikebana* was also used to adorn the royal palaces and the houses of the nobility. Later still *ikebana* spread to the homes of ordinary people and today it is one of the most graceful traditions of Japanese life.

Bonsai is the art of arranging plants into certain shapes and is the Japanese word literally meaning 'tray-planted'. It is an older art than *ikebana* and first began in China. *Ikebana* uses fresh flowers and other decorative material such as twigs, mosses and leaves. Bonsai is the art of growing fully developed trees in miniature. This is done by keeping them to a small size while still making them look like real trees. It is a very difficult art and requires a great deal of patience and time. To produce a dwarf tree between 30 and 40 centimetres high can take up to 100 years of careful work. The art of bonsai is passed on from father to son and one tree can be handed down from one generation to the next as a valued possession.

A Chinese juniper which is 200 years old and about 90 cm. high

Where ginger is produced

The ginger plant was used in India and China in very ancient times. By the first century A.D. it had travelled to the Mediterranean region and it was well-known in England by the eleventh century. Today it is grown in all the tropical regions of the world.

The essential oils and gums found in the ginger plant are used as stimulants in certain drugs. Ginger is used by doctors, in the manufacture of beverages and as a spice in cooking.

The ginger plant is propagated by cuttings of the rhizome, or root. Nine or ten months after planting, the stems turn yellow and wither and the ginger is then ready to be gathered. Green ginger, used in cooking, is the fresh rhizome. Pieces of rhizome can be washed

Ring-necked pheasant (*Phasianus colchicus*)

Golden pheasant (*Chrisolophus pictus*)

and then dried in the sun before use, or they can be peeled before being dried.

Where the pheasant first came from

The pheasant, a beautiful bird often sought by hunters, first lived in the mountainous region of the Caucasus. The ancient Romans brought it to Europe.

In its natural state the pheasant likes to make its home in moist woodlands, especially on hillsides. The cock, or male, has brightly coloured feathers which have a metallic sheen. The hen, or female, is plainer, and is of a brownish colour. Both male and female have very long tails.

Many varieties occur in different parts of Asia, the Japanese green pheasant being particularly notable. In Europe, pheasants are often bred as game birds for sport.

Where the Great Wall of China was built

This gigantic fortification was designed as a defensive barrier to protect the Chinese empire against attacks from invading hordes of barbarians. The Great Wall was built along the northern border of China from about 200 B.C. Local feudal lords had already built some walls and forts many years previously in places such as gaps in the mountains where enemy soldiers could easily slip through into China. It was not until the great emperor Shih Huang Ti who reigned from 221 to 210 B.C. that all these walls and forts were linked up and extended as one barrier.

The Great Wall reached a length of about 2,400 kilometres, the longest wall ever built, winding its way up mountains and down into valleys. The height of the wall ranges from 6 to 16 metres and along its top there used to be a road more than 4 metres wide. Every so often there was a huge tower where soldiers lived and kept guard.

Chinese costumes

The Great Wall of China was repaired and improved in later years. Today it is mostly in ruins. The government of the People's Republic of China has rebuilt sections and many tourists go to admire these great structures.

Where the Ainu live

In the Japanese islands of Hokkaido, Sakhalin and Kuril lives a group of people who are unlike the vast majority of people in Japan. These are the Ainu. They do not have slanting eyes, a yellow skin or wiry, black hair, but they look more like Europeans, with a light-coloured skin and thick hair. The men usually have heavy beards which are not very common in Japan.

The Ainu may be descendants of early Caucasoid peoples, that is the group to which most Europeans belong. They are known as aborigines because anthropologists believe they were the first inhabitants of Japan before the Koreans and other yellow-skinned people came to the country during the Stone Age. The Ainu may have reached Japan from the West in prehistoric times.

The original Ainu speech had no known connection with any other language, but today it has been largely replaced by Japanese. The Ainu live in small villages, leading a very simple life, hunting, fishing and gardening. Their numbers are greatly reduced and they seem to be dying out except where they have intermarried with Japanese.

Where the most beautiful gentian in the world grows

There are about 400 varieties of the gentian plant. Some grow quite tall, with yellow or purple flowers, and some have pale blue flowers. There are also acaulescent types which have little or no stems and are the best-known with their deep or brilliant blue flowers, and gentians with branches that have small bunches of flowers.

Oddly enough gentians do not grow in Africa, but they are common in other parts of the world, especially in the highlands of the Himalayas. In these regions are found some of the most beautiful and rare types of gentians.

In Europe, gentians grow on the Alps. Ten species of gentian are found in Britain.

Gentiana sind-ornata

Ainu costumes

Where rice is more important than wheat

There are hundreds of millions of people in the world who have never tasted a piece of bread. This is because their main food is rice. They live chiefly in eastern Asia, in such countries as India, China, Japan and the islands of Indonesia.

In the warm, humid regions of the tropics, farmers harvest the rice twice a year to help feed the many millions for whom this grain is their staple food. Farmers have grown rice in China and India for over 4,000 years. Gradually the cultivation of rice spread and it was introduced to Europe in mediaeval times by the Arabs.

Rice grows as small grains from the flower of the rice plant. Each grain has special layers of protective covering which are removed when the rice is polished and turned into a white grain. Rice is rich in starch, a vital substance in feeding the human body, and also contains other important substance such as vitamins. These vitamins are found inside the protective layers of rice grains, so when the grains are polished the vitamins are lost. In some places in Asia where many people eat a lot of polished rice, they do not receive these vitamins and so suffer from diseases which make them weak through vitamin deficiency.

In China people eat rice with pork, chicken, beef or fish, the meat being cut into small pieces and flavoured with soya sauce or spicy gravy; in India rice is eaten in a curry made with powdered spices, meat and vegetables; in Japan the people eat rice with fried or raw fish and chopped, raw vegetables.

A farmer in his rice field

The picturesque Irawadi rice-boat

Gibbons

Where to find gibbons

The dense forests of tropical Asia often echo to the hoarse, piercing, far-reaching cries of the gibbon. This is a small, man-like ape or monkey which is quite common in the East, especially in Indo-Malayan countries.

It is not difficult to recognize gibbons because they have certain striking characteristics. The chief of these is their extremely long arms. When a gibbon stands up on its hind legs it can still touch the ground with its fingertips, for its arms are about twice as long as its legs.

The gibbon has a slender body covered in brown fur, but no tail. It is an extremely muscular animal and a marvellous acrobat, swinging from branch to branch of the trees with considerable skill and agility.

Sometimes gibbons jump great distances between trees. They can also hang for a very long time with one hand from a branch while swinging gracefully to and fro like a pendulum.

They feed on young bamboo shoots, nuts, fruit, insects and birds' eggs, and live mainly in the trees. When on the ground they walk upright, without any help from their long arms, which are held above their heads or behind them.

Siamese costumes

Where bonzes live

Buddhist priests are usually known as bonzes. In recent years they have become familiar figures throughout the world, chiefly through their activities in connection with the Vietnam war. On 11 June 1963, a bonze named Quang Duc burned himself to death in a square in Saigon, the capital of South Vietnam. The bonze soaked his robes in petrol and then set light to himself in protest against what he believed was the corrupt government of the country. Many other bonzes followed Duc's example and a wave of horror swept the world at what was happening in this unfortunate Asian country.

Only then did many people

learn about bonzes who, dressed in their saffron-coloured robes, were dedicated to prayer and meditation. Bonzes have a very long history that dates back to the first preachings of the Buddhist religion in the sixth century B.C.

Today there are bonzes in all regions of Asia. Their religion was born in India as an offshoot of the Hindu religion, and was carried to Sri Lanka, formerly called Ceylon, to Afghanistan and to all central Asia. From about A.D. 100, the Buddhist religion spread to China, Japan, Tibet, Indo-China and later still to the Indonesian islands.

Outside Asia Buddhists are found in North and South America and in Europe. There are over 168 million Buddhists alive today in various parts of the world.

Where the first atomic bomb fell

In 1945 the Allies launched stronger attacks against Japan. Because of the greater combat range of the B-29 bomber, the aeroplane known as the 'flying fortress', the Americans were able to carry out air raids every day on Japanese territory. The cities of Japan were very densely populated and many of the houses were made of wood. When the bombs fell these buildings burned like tinder. In the last few months of the Second World War, from March 1945, American aeroplanes dropped many tons of fire bombs on the principal Japanese cities. About 250,000 people were killed in these air raids and houses over an area of more than 450 square kilometres were burned to the ground. On the night of 9 March 1945, American B-29 bombers from air bases in the Marianne Islands in the Pacific Ocean flew at almost 1,500 metres above Tokyo and devastated the Japanese capital with fire bombs. In that one night alone almost 38 square kilometres of the city was burned to the ground.

On 6 August 1945, a B-29 bomber dropped one solitary bomb on the city of Hiroshima. The bomb was light compared with some of the huge bombs previously dropped on enemy cities, but this was

Hiroshima

an atomic bomb and its terrible explosive power was the same as 20,000 tons of the explosive T.N.T. going off. The first atomic bomb destroyed 60 per cent of Hiroshima and killed about 80,000 men, women and children. Three days later the city of Nagasaki was attacked with a second and larger atomic bomb. The effects of these bombs were terrible. The two explosions brought an end to the world war which had raged for almost six years.

Where to find the 'waters that purify'

The Ganges is the sacred river for the people of India who believe that its waters have been blessed by God to cleanse and purify any person who bathes in them and has faith. Every year millions of Hindu pilgrims bathe in the waters of the Ganges, believing the purification will affect not only themselves but their children and their children's children as far as the seventh generation. When Hindus die their bodies are cremated and their ashes scattered on the Ganges.

The Ganges is about 2,700 kilometres long. The larger of its two main headstreams rises near the Tibetan border; the smaller begins in a cave of ice on the southern slopes of the Himalayas. Many tributaries flow into it, including the Jumna which is 1,376 kilometres long. The Ganges flows steadily for much of its course. Its waters come from the glaciers in the Himalayas and from the torrential rain brought by the monsoon winds.

The valley of the Ganges is one of the most fertile and densely populated regions of India. The river flows through the holy city of Benares, the capital, New Delhi, and the large city of Calcutta, before emptying into the Bay of Bengal.

Before it reaches the sea, the Ganges joins with another great river, the Brahmaputra, forming a delta which is criss-crossed with waterways and covered mainly by dense jungle.

Where nutmegs come from

Nutmeg is a spice which, grated into powder, is often used in cooking to flavour meat or cakes. The nutmeg is the seed of a tree that grows in the Moluccas and in the Philippines, both groups of islands in the Pacific Ocean. Farmers also grow the nutmeg tree in warm regions such as India, Indo-China and in the West Indies and tropical regions of America.

The nutmeg tree is an evergreen and can reach up to 20 metres high. It yields fruit when it is about eight years old and continues to do so for sixty years or more. The tree needs a warm, moist climate and grows much better if it is near the sea. It also requires much care and attention and the right type of soil to grow in.

Every year the nutmeg tree produces thousands of oval fruits covered in a thin yellow skin. As the fruits ripen, the skin splits open and reveals the seed. The nutmegs are gathered and dried before being sold.

The *Mala pansi*, a small Ganges sailing craft

Vietnamese girl

Where to find the people who have always been at war

Vietnam, with Laos and Cambodia, forms part of the peninsula of Indo-China. From 1862 to 1893 French soldiers conquered the area and divided it into five regions: Tonkin, Annam, Cochin China, Cambodia and Laos. In 1941 Japanese soldiers invaded Indo-China and occupied the region for five years, during which the people suffered greatly. After the defeat of the Japanese in the Second World War, the French returned to Indo-China in 1946 but the Vietnamese wanted to rule themselves and formed bands of guerrillas to fight the French troops. By 1954 these guerrillas had driven the French soldiers away from many parts of the country. The French were finally defeated in 1954 after the siege of Dien Bien Phu. After the defeat an international conference was held in Geneva, which gave independence to Laos and Cambodia and divided Vietnam into two parts along the line of the seventeenth parallel. The guerrillas had liberated most of the northern part of the country except for an area around Hanoi and the mouth of the Red River. Fighting among the guerrillas continued and from 1954 the United States sent troops to Vietnam to help the government of South Vietnam to fight the guerrillas. The war was very fierce but the United States was unable to defeat the guerrillas and in 1973 American troops were being withdrawn from Vietnam.

The Thomson ·45 calibre sub-machine gun

Where the Phoenician civilization flourished

The Phoenicians were a people who, from about 2700 B.C., lived in the region that is now Lebanon that stretched between the mountains in the east and the Mediterranean Sea in the west. The Phoenicians had no large, fertile plains to farm and they decided to seek their fortune on the seas. They became the most skilful sailors of ancient times.

The forests of Lebanon, rich in lofty cedars, provided the Phoenicians with the wood to build their sailing ships and war fleets. They travelled to all parts of the Mediterranean Sea, sailing close to the coasts of the countries they passed, and even reached the Pillars of Hercules, a place now known as the Straits of Gibraltar.

The Phoenicians founded the city of Cadiz on the Atlantic coast of Spain where they built a magnificent temple full of rich and sacred objects.

During their early sea voyages the Phoenicians navigated by the pole star. Their fame as navigators became so great that Pharaoh Necho II of Egypt, ordered them to sail all round Africa which they did in about 600 B.C.

The Cedar of Lebanon (*Cedrus Libani*)

Where the monsoon winds blow

Monsoons are winds that blow during certain seasons of the year in southern Asia, parts of Africa, northern Australia and parts of North and South America.

They are caused by the difference of the temperatures of the land and the ocean. The monsoon blows from cold towards warmer regions: in summer, cool air travels to the land from the sea and meets warmer air; in winter, the cool air travels from the land and meets the warmer air over the sea.

In southern Asia, the monsoon winds blow from the Indian Ocean to as far as Tibet and back again. The path of monsoon winds is sometimes changed by the rotation of the Earth which makes the winds follow a curved path. In summer, when the monsoon winds blow from the sea to the land, they carry vast quantities of moisture produced by the strong heat of the sun on the sea. The moisture appears as huge clouds which gather at the foot of the Himalaya mountain range and down into the plains of northern India. These clouds produce the torrential downpours which go on for a long time during the monsoon season. The heavy rainfall stops only when the monsoon winds change direction and blow back towards the sea again.

This change of direction frequently produces stormy weather with terrible, destructive winds called typhoons and tornadoes.

Where to find the 'Venice of the East'

Thailand is an ancient kingdom in eastern Asia that was known as Siam until 1948. Its capital city, Bangkok, is a beautiful place situated on the banks of the river Maenam, about 33 kilometres from the sea. Bangkok is crisscrossed by many canals which have won the city the name of 'Venice of the East'. Bangkok is also famous for its gardens and the hundreds of pagodas, tall, ornamental towers. The canals of the city are thronged with people on sampans, the traditional boat of Thailand, which are used to carry goods, and as shops and even homes for families.

About a fifth of the population of Bangkok lives on the waterways, working, trading, shopping, cooking, eating and sleeping on sampans. Few of the streets and modern buildings are more than fifty years old for it was only after 1900 that most of the modern buildings were constructed.

Bangkok has several hundred Buddhist temples. Among the most famous are Wat Pho which has a huge gilded reclining Buddha, and the marble temple of Wat Benchamabopit. The vast Grand Palace includes the Dusit throne hall and the king's chapel which contains a sacred jasper image of Buddha. These shrines are one reason why Bangkok attracts about 10,000 tourists a year.

The Pechili trading junk

Where the Bedouin live

Today the word 'Arab' means any person who lives in a group of countries in western Asia or northern Africa such as Egypt, Algeria or Jordan. But the true Arabs are a people who live in the Arabian peninsula, across the Red Sea from Africa. These people have no fixed homes. They are called nomads because they wander from place to place with their herds of goats, sheep or camels. In fact, the word 'Arab' means 'nomad' in Arabic. These nomadic people are known as the Bedouin. They live in a region called in Arabic *bajia*, that is a vast plain with very little vegetation. Although the Bedouin make up about one-tenth of the total population of the Middle East, they occupy nearly nine-tenths of its area.

It is very difficult to trace the origins of the Bedouin. They have never learned to read or write and so have kept no records of their past. In the days of the ancient Romans the Bedouin frequently raided the coastal regions. The Romans had to build many forts to stand up to these attacks. The Bedouin used to gather together every so often in major centres of the Arab world such as Aleppo, Mecca and Hormuz. It was at these gatherings that Mahomet, the prophet who is today honoured by Moslems all over the world as the founder of the Islamic religion, first preached his religious teachings.

The Bedouin live a difficult life. The Arabian desert where they live is extremely hot and water is very scarce as rain does not fall for several years in certain parts. The Bedouin therefore have to keep moving to look for food for themselves and their animals. They live in tents and breed camels which they sell at markets for such foods as barley and dates. With the coming of industry to Arabia following the discovery of oil, many Bedouin have given up their wandering life and taken jobs on oilfields.

Where the emperors are regarded as divine

The word 'Japan' means the land of the rising sun. There is an old legend which links the fortunes of this beautiful and graceful country with its emperors. The legend relates that in the far distant past the god Izanagi and the goddess Izanami distributed the government of the world and surrounding space among other gods and goddesses. Amaterasu, the goddess of the sun, became the ruler of the heavens. Her brother, Susanowo, the god of storms, was made the ruler of the seas.

The brother and sister did not get on well with one another. Amaterasu was gentle and kind; Susanowo was violent and spiteful. In the end poor Amaterasu ran away from her brother's bad temper and hid herself in a cave. Darkness fell upon the world. Izanagi and Izanami were very sad and devised a plan to bring Amaterasu back. On a tree that grew outside the cave they hung a necklace and a mirror. Amaterasu was rather vain and she slipped out of the cave to look at herself in the mirror and to try on the necklace. Izanagi and Izanami seized her and sunshine came back to the world.

Susanowo the troublemaker was punished and the gods sent

him away into exile. He wandered all over the world waiting to be forgiven. One day he went to Japan where he killed a fierce dragon that had eight tails and eight heads and had been terrorizing the country for eight years. Inside one of the tails Susanowo found a beautiful sword. He decided to give the sword to his sister and to ask her forgiveness. Amaterasu was very kind-hearted. She accepted the sword and forgave Susanowo and happiness returned to the world.

Then Amaterasu's nephew came down from the sky. He took the necklace and the mirror and became the first emperor of Japan. The old legend says that all the Japanese emperors since then were descended from him and for this reason the people regarded their rulers as divine or godlike.

In Japan today, the necklace (symbolizing benevolence), the mirror (purity) and the sword (courage) are the symbols of the emperor's power and authority and are known as the three sacred treasures.

Where lychees grow

The lychee is a small, evergreen tree about 6 metres high which for thousands of years farmers in China have cultivated. It was later grown in South Africa, the Hawaiian Islands and parts of America.

In China the fruit of the lychee tree is a very popular delicacy and people prefer them to oranges or peaches. The lychee fruit is about the same size as a small plum, oval to round in shape with a hard, brittle skin which is strawberry-red in colour when ripe.

The white, translucent, juicy flesh of the lychee has a delicious, refreshing taste resembling that of a muscatel grape.

Where to find the yurts of the Mongolians

Until the eighteenth century the Mongols were mainly a nomadic, or wandering people. They were also fierce warriors who ruled over a vast territory of central Asia. Throughout the extensive plains of this region they built round tents called yurts, constructed of collapsible wooden frames covered with felt, which were easily folded and transported to new places.

The Mongols reached the height of their power under the leadership of Genghis Khan during the early thirteenth century when hordes of Mongols invaded and pillaged northern China. Later they went to Russia and rode as far as Budapest in Hungary.

Mongolia is now divided into two areas: Inner Mongolia, which is a self-governing region within the People's Republic of China, and Outer Mongolia, called the Mongolian People's Republic. Only a few of the people who still wander in the plains live in yurts.

Elephants carrying logs of teak in a Burmese forest

Where to find teak

Teak is wood obtained from a type of tree known as *Tectona*. It is one of the most valuable woods because it is extremely hard and durable and can withstand the attacks of insects which bore holes into other kinds of wood and spoil them. The strength of teak comes from an essential oil present in the wood.

Tectona trees grow only in the dense forests of equatorial regions. It is difficult to transport the trees from these forests and for this reason teak is very expensive.

Burma produces most of the world's supply of teak, with India, Thailand, Java and Sri Lanka (formerly Ceylon) coming next.

Teak trees grow to an average height of 20 metres, although mature trees of 100 years old or more can reach 30 to 40 metres. The bark of the tree is about a centimetre thick and is brownish-grey in colour. The sapwood is white and beneath this is the heartwood which has a strong aromatic fragrance and is a golden brown colour, which on seasoning darkens to brown marked with darker streaks.

In warm countries teak is chiefly valued for its durability. Well-preserved teak beams have been found in buildings several centuries old and there are even instances of teak beams having lasted for more than 1,000 years.

Teak is used in building ships and houses and also for fine furniture and wood carvings. A great deal of teak is shaved into very thin slices, called veneers, which are stuck to furniture made from other, cheaper woods. It was once used to make the decks of sailing ships because it did not rot as easily as other woods. Today it has become very popular in furniture-making but most of the woods sold as teak are really imitations that look like the original.

Where the persimmon came from

Until the nineteenth century the persimmon was almost unknown in Europe. Today this yellowish-red fruit which looks rather like a tomato, is often seen in homes in Mediterranean countries such as France and Italy. It is also grown on a small scale in the United States.

The persimmon is a native of China and Japan where it has grown since ancient times. Persimmon trees soon became accustomed to the Mediterranean weather when they were first brought to Europe during the nineteenth century. The trees have dark-green leaves and are often planted in gardens where they give shade against the hot summer sun.

Persimmon fruit is no longer as popular as it was, but the wood from the tree is used in making furniture and looks like ebony.

Where the tiger likes to make its home

The jungles and the forests of Asia which have rivers flowing through them are the favourite haunts of the tiger, one of the fiercest and most dangerous animals in the world.

Unlike the lion, this beautiful big cat with the striped yellow coat is not satisfied to kill just one animal for its food. It will attack whole flocks of animals as they drink at waterholes in the jungle, slaughtering them for the sheer pleasure of killing and spilling blood.

As the tiger grows older it becomes weaker and more dangerous and will then attack human beings and become a man-eater. Once a tiger has tasted human flesh it will always want more, attacking any person who strays too far into the jungle from the villages. Man-eating tigers will even break into houses to seize their human victims.

Where jute, kapok and ramie are found

Jute is a substance obtained from various plants that grow in warm and moist regions of Asia. It is cheap and used in making rope, twine and material for sacks.

Kapok is a fluffy substance from the outer covering of certain tropical plants. The most common of these is the *Ceiba pentandra*, a tree that is grown mainly in Indonesia and produces hundreds of football-shaped pods. Kapok is very light and soft and is used as stuffing for sleeping-bags, cushions and mattresses.

Ramie is a very strong material obtained from the stalks of plants belonging to the nettle family. It was grown in ancient Egypt where it was used to wrap mummies, and is native to China and Formosa. Today it is used in fire hose, fishing nets and upholstery.

Where birds help to keep the streets clean

Marabous belong to the stork family and are often seen in the equatorial regions of Asia. They are also known as 'adjutant birds' because of the way they stand to attention like soldiers.

These birds are not very fussy about what they eat and enjoy almost any kind of refuse. For this reason they crowd together in villages and do the useful job of clearing the streets of any rubbish that is lying around. Marabous will also eat the rotting bodies of dead animals, often quarrelling with other carrion birds such as vultures and fighting over pieces of stinking, rotten meat.

With such eating habits the marabou cannot be described as an attractive bird. It has an enormous beak about 40 centimetres long; a tiny head with no feathers on it; and a long, curved neck, also bare and covered with a very rough skin, which is usually kept tucked between its shoulders. The front of the neck contains a loose pouch which the bird keeps stuffed with food. Marabous are up to one and a half metres tall when they stand up straight on their long legs.

Egyptian vulture (left) and marabou

Where bananas first grew

The bananas we see on sale in greengrocer shops today come mainly from warm countries in the American continent. But the banana is not a native fruit of America: until 1500 nobody in America had ever seen one. The ancient Greeks knew about bananas which they found when they marched eastwards into Asia in the army of Alexander the Great. The banana plant was taken to America when that continent was discovered in 1492. America now provides the world with most of its bananas. Ecuador, a country in South America, is one of the largest producers.

The banana plant is not a tree but a kind of giant herb that grows up to 9 metres high. The plant grows very quickly and takes only a year to develop and produce fruit. The plant then dies but as it withers away another plant grows from its underground stem. In this way bananas keep growing on new stems throughout the year.

Where hamsters come from

At one time hamsters lived wild on the broad plains of central Europe. Today their natural home is in western Asia in a region between Syria and Israel.

Hamsters are bred as pets. They are also used in scientific experiments in laboratories together with rats and guinea pigs. In their natural state they live in large families, digging a maze of tunnels under the ground where they live and store their food. Farmers do not like hamsters because these little creatures can do serious damage to field crops.

Hamsters have two roomy pouches inside their jaws. When they find food they stuff their pouches full with it and take it back to their nests to store for future use.

Hamsters are rodents which means they have two long sharp teeth at the front of their mouths with which they gnaw their food in the same way as mice and rabbits.

Where to find the earthquake islands

In some regions of the Earth the crust, or top layer, is weak. Sometimes the crust cracks and this causes a terrible movement of the ground known as an earthquake. Regions prone to these cracks are known as seismic areas. The best-known seismic area is the so-called firebelt of the Pacific Ocean. This zone has a long chain of volcanoes which belch out smoke and contain molten rock known as lava. The seismic area includes the islands of Japan.

Usually these earthquakes are very mild and do little or no damage, for modern buildings in Japanese cities are built to stand up to even severe earth tremors.

Some earthquakes, however, can bring disaster. On 1 September 1923 a violent earthquake struck Tokyo, resulting in the death of an estimated 74,000 people and leaving 64 per cent of the surviving population homeless.

Ruins in Tokyo after the earthquake of 1923

Where to find the sacred gavial

Indian crocodile (*Gavialis gangeticus*)

The gavial is a type of crocodile some 4 to 5 metres long, that lives in the river Ganges in India and is quite different from the crocodile of the river Nile in Egypt. Although it belongs to the same order of reptiles, it forms a family of its own, the Gavialidae.

The distinguishing characteristic of the gavial is its very long, slender jaws that swell out into a bump at the end and this is where the nose is. This nose enables the gavial to breathe while the rest of its body is completely under the water.

The gavial has rows of sharp, equal-sized teeth which look very frightening when it opens its jaws wide. But this is not a dangerous creature and will not attack people or animals who may approach it on the river banks. It prefers to eat dead animals and fish which it catches with quick sideways movements of its head.

Many people in south-eastern Asia believe that the gavial is sacred. In some places gavials are kept in the grounds of temples and looked after with great care and respect.

Where to find the salt-water crocodile

The crocodile of the river Nile in Egypt is well known as a fierce reptile which will attack large animals and even people. But the Nile crocodile is not as fierce and hungry a creature as the salt-water crocodile which lives along the shores of Asia between the Bay of Bengal and the southern coasts of China.

The salt-water crocodile is larger than the Nile crocodile and can grow to a length of nearly 6 metres. It is bloodthirsty and voracious and fiercer than a tiger.

In the water it is very dangerous because it can swim extremely fast and its victims rarely know of the danger until it is too late.

Where the mango grows

The mango is a fruit that first grew in southern Asia. Today it is grown in any part of the world that has a warm, tropical climate.

The mango tree can grow to a height of 20 metres and has long evergreen leaves which make it one of the favourite shade trees of the tropics. There are many varieties of mango and the fruit varies considerably in size and character. The smallest mangoes are the size of plums while others can weigh as much as 2 kilogrammes. They can be oval, round, kidney-shaped or long and thin and vary in colour from red to yellow or green. The soft yellow flesh is juicy with a delicious spicy flavour and surrounds a large, flattened seed.

Mangoes must be eaten soon after gathering because they go bad within a few days.

Where cormorants help fishermen

There are about thirty species of cormorant, a long-necked sea-bird which is found all over the world. The cormorant lives in colonies together with thousands of other birds along rocky coasts. These huge flocks of birds leave large deposits of droppings known as guano on the rocks, and this is used as fertilizer by farmers. The greatest producers of guano are the cormorants of Peru.

Cormorants never go far out to sea for they have short wings and do not fly very well. But they are excellent divers: as soon as a cormorant sees a fish darting about in the waves, it plunges into the sea and re-appears later with a fish wriggling about in its long, hook-tipped beak. Cormorants can stay under water without breathing for more than two minutes, gobbling up many small fish which they store inside a part of their neck known as the gullet. When their gullets are full of fish the cormorants go back to their nests on the rocks where they bring up the fish they have swallowed and feed them to their babies.

Fishermen all over the world dislike cormorants because they are very greedy birds, always trying to steal fish from the nets and baskets of fishing boats. But the fishermen of China are glad of these birds which they catch. The fishermen then put a ring round the bird's neck and tie a long cord to it, like a lead to a dog's collar. The cormorant is then allowed to dive into the sea and catch fish; but it cannot swallow them because the ring round the bird's neck stops the fish from going down its throat. The fisherman then pulls the bird back to the boat where it drops the fish it has caught.

When cormorants work like this they are always kept hungry so that they will catch even more fish. The birds are so skilful that a boat with six cormorants can return to port with all its baskets full of fish after only a few hours.

When cormorants come back from diving in the sea, they sit on rocks and flap their wings gently to dry their feathers which are not waterproof as the feathers of most other sea-birds.

Where to find the pangolin

This very strange mammal lives in the dense equatorial jungles of Asia and is common in the islands of Malaysia. Another type of pangolin makes its home in the forests of Africa.

The pangolin is a shy, harmless, nocturnal animal with a long body up to a metre in length which resembles the anteater. It has a small head, short legs and a thick tail which is always curled up like a question mark. The skin of its throat and the underparts of the body is soft, but the rest of the pangolin's body is covered in hard, horny, yellowish-brown scales which are so made that the pangolin can roll itself up into a ball when it is frightened or in danger.

The name 'pangolin' comes from a Javanese word meaning 'the animal that rolls up into a ball'. The pangolin, which has no teeth, uses its long, sticky, snake-like tongue to scoop up ants and termites, insects that provide its only food. The pangolin also has very strong claws on its forefeet, but it uses these only for tearing down anthills to force the insects out into the open ground.

Pangolin

Where the dugong lives

This strange, seal-like mammal lives along the coast of the Red Sea, the Indian Ocean and in the China seas. A long time ago fishermen who saw the dugong thought that this animal looked rather like a woman and behaved strangely like a human being, shedding real tears and whimpering and sobbing when caught. The fishermen's tales about the dugong were soon spread round the world and people kept adding more details until the myth was born that the dugong had the head and body of a woman and a long fish-tail. Perhaps this was how all the old beliefs about mermaids and sirens began. In olden days sailors believed that mermaids sang sweetly to seamen on passing ships and tried to lure the ships on to dangerous rocks.

In actual fact the dugong belongs to the order of animals known as *Sirenia*. It is from 2 to 3 metres in length and browses in small groups in the shallow waters of bays and inlets. When feeding underwater it surfaces every five to ten minutes for a supply of air. People on the coast often hunt the dugong with spears or harpoons for its flesh is considered a delicacy. Oil is obtained from its blubber.

Dugong

Where opium is grown

Opium is one of the most frequently used drugs in the world, especially in the East where it is smoked or chewed. It is obtained from the milky juice of a poppy known as *Papaver somniferum*, the 'sleep-bringing poppy'. When the milky juice is extracted from the poppy it turns dark when

A woman from Anatolia

exposed to the light and becomes hard. The hardened juice is then rolled into balls and sent to refineries where it is prepared for medical uses.

Opium is a narcotic drug, easing pain and helping people to sleep, but it is also a dangerous drug because people who take it can soon become addicted.

Where to find the sacred volcano

The people of Japan regard the extinct volcano of Fujiyama as a holy mountain. Fujiyama stands on the island of Honshu and rises to a height of 3,776 metres, its snow-covered peak dominating the surrounding countryside.

An old legend says Fujiyama was born in a single night about 300 years before the birth of Christ. As the volcano rose from the ground the earth a few hundred kilometres away collapsed to form Lake Biwa.

Every year many thousands of pilgrims climb to the top of Fujiyama. They throw gifts into the vast crater to please the gods of the underworld who are believed to be responsible for the many earthquakes so feared in Japan.

Where to find the Chinese alligator

Many alligators live in the great rivers that flow across China and are especially common in the lower reaches of the Yangtze Kiang. These alligators look different from the crocodile because they have shorter jaws. The fourth tooth of the Chinese alligator's upper jaw is also large and sticks out when the animal has its mouth closed.

The American alligator which lives in the Mississippi River grows to about 6 metres in length, but the Chinese alligator is rarely longer than one and a half metres. It is too timid to attack large animals and presents no danger to human beings. It prefers, instead, to catch fish, water-birds and small mammals.

79

Kurdistan costumes

Where the Kurds live

The Kurds are a brave and proud people who originally came from the mountains that lie between the Caucasus and Turkey. They were the only people in western Asia to defeat the fierce armies of Mongols who invaded the area from eastern Asia.

Today the Kurds are nomads, or wandering shepherds, skilled craftsmen and brave fighters. They practise the Moslem religion and follow closely the traditional ways of their people. This respect for tradition is a common bond that links Kurds wherever they are living between Armenia and Iran.

At one time the Kurds were an independent people, especially in the Turkish Ottoman empire. During the 1960s they demanded a state of their own: their demands were refused and this led to violent revolts. Two of these revolts, in 1961 and 1966, were against the government of Iran and many Kurds lost their lives in the fighting.

Where the fig is held sacred

The pagoda fig is regarded as a sacred tree in India where it grows wild. The seeds of this fig tree are often dropped by birds, squirrels, monkeys or fruit-eating bats on to other trees. When the fig seed has landed on a tree it pushes out a root with the help of heat from the sun and moisture in the air. This root grows down attached to the trunk of the supporting plant until it reaches the ground where it becomes embedded. When this has happened the sacred fig tree is born and soon its branches and leaves appear.

Every branch then produces its own root which grows down to the soil and the whole process is repeated. After a while the fig seed has produced hundreds of trees all linked together by their branches.

In the meantime, the tree on which the first seed fell has died of suffocation. Pagoda fig trees continue to spread for many years, producing a forest of their own of thousands of trunks.

Where the Baluchi live

The Baluchi are a wandering people known as nomads. They live in small tribes in the vast high tablelands between Iran and West Pakistan. The tablelands are bordered in the south by the Arabian Sea at the Gulf of Oman. This region is known as Baluchistan and is called after the people who live in it. Baluchistan is crossed by several chains of mountains which rise to a height of more than 2,000 metres in places. These mountains enclose broad areas of desert that contain scattered salt lakes.

The Baluchi are a poor people. They practise the Islamic religion and live in tents, wandering through the desolate, windswept desert in search of grazing grounds for the camels, cattle, sheep and goats which represent their only form of wealth. Some Baluchi now have a more settled existence, living in villages of mud or stone huts.

The Baluchi tribes are skilful at carpet-weaving and embroidery and they also make woollen goods. They sell these goods to travellers passing through the desert in caravans. Carpets made by the Baluchi people often fetch high prices when sold in European markets.

Baluchistan costumes

Where to find the archerfish

There are several species of archerfish but the best known lives in the fresh waters of Java and the other islands of the Malay archipelago. It is about 15 to 20 centimetres long and is a beautiful silvery-green colour. The archerfish has an unusual way of catching its food: it actually shoots its prey.

The people of Java hold contests in which these fish compete against each other in shooting matches. The Javanese place a stick in the centre of a tank with the top of the stick about a metre above the surface of the water. They then put various insects on hooks at the top of the stick. As the archerfish swim in the water they see the insects; then they poke their heads above the surface, carefully take aim and shoot out a thin jet of water. When this hits the target the insect falls down and the archerfish gobbles it up.

If the archerfish misses with its first shot it swims round the tank once more, takes aim and sends out another jet of water. The archerfish can shoot a jet of water up to a distance of one and a half metres. This fish can shoot water because of a small hole at the front of its head. When it wants to shoot an insect it closes its gills very tightly. This forces the water into the little hole and the fish uses its thin and very flexible tongue to push the water out.

The victims of the archerfish are usually the insects that skim along the surface of the water near the shore.

Archer fish (*Toxotes jaculator*)

THE WHERE OF NORTH AND CENTRAL AMERICA

English and Indian trappers

Where the fur hunters of America tracked their prey

The fur hunters and trappers of America explored the vast areas of the northern part of the continent. These hunters were rough and ready and during the 1600s they hunted fur animals in places where no other white man had ever set foot, defying wild Indians who lived there and showing no fear of the many dangers that surrounded them.

The greatest hunting ground was Canada. It was so rich in fur animals that the British fought the French to win possession of this huge country. In 1670 the British had set up the Hudson's Bay Company and in 1821 this company incorporated its rival, so gaining a monopoly of all the fur trade.

From about 1820 the valley of the river Missouri in the United States and the region of the Rocky Mountains became important hunting areas. These places were explored by the 'mountain men' led by General Ashley who was the first to establish the American fur trade on a permanent basis in the Rockies. These men helped to open up the Wild West for settlers to go and farm there.

Where to find the world's most famous waterfalls

The most famous waterfalls in the world are at Niagara. Some 500,000 tons of water rush over the Niagara precipice into a gorge below every minute and make this one of the best sources of hydroelectric power in America. The dull roar of the waters can be heard from a great distance. The people who live near the falls are used to the sound and would be quite nervous if it should suddenly stop. This almost happened one night in March 1848 when the waters of the river Niagara were blocked by huge masses of ice and the great falls were reduced to a trickle for a few hours.

There are two falls at Niagara and they are separated by a huge rock, called Goat Island. The larger of the falls is in Canada and the other is in the United States. Engineers have bored a tunnel in the rock through which people can go to see the marvellous spectacle. The falls are very beautiful in winter because of the ice round them. They are visited by over 4 million sightseers a year.

Where the winged lizards lived

In the days of the dinosaurs the sky was crowded with huge winged reptiles such as the pterodactyl. These flying reptiles had a wing span of more than 7 metres and would constantly glide above the waters, catching fish and crab-like animals. They were excellent fliers and could travel over 100 kilometres away from the land in search of their food.

Pterodactyl

Pterodactyls were probably the most skilful fliers of the winged reptiles, but their huge wings were a hindrance to them whenever they landed to rest. At such times the pterodactyl would have to drag itself painfully along the ground in contrast to its agility and grace in the air.

The fossil remains of the pterodactyl have been found in several parts of North America. This means that these flying lizards must have lived in that part of the world.

Where to find the most majestic valley in the world

There is a region in the United States where erosion by water and wind has produced a majestic effect. This area forms part of three states: Arizona, Utah and Nevada. The river which has carved out such beauty is called the Colorado. The waters of the Colorado empty into the Pacific Ocean but before they finish their journey they pass through a valley that has steep sides. This valley was cut out of the earth by the Colorado River over a period of millions of years.

The valleys consist of a series of canyons which all lead to the magnificent Grand Canyon. In some places the valley is more than 1,600 metres deep and 25 kilometres wide. The canyon presents a breathtaking sight with its red walls rising sheer out of the ground. Where the various valleys meet, isolated peaks rise out of deep depressions. During the wet season torrential rains flood the Colorado River when its waters rise by more than 40 metres, and the mass of soil it contains is constantly reshaping the walls of the Grand Canyon.

Where to find the world's tallest trees

On the mountains of the Sierra Nevada in places that are carefully protected, grow the world's tallest trees: the sequoias. Sequoias are famous for their tremendous height and for their great age. Some of the tallest and the oldest of these trees are so famous that they have their own special names and are looked after very carefully.

There are two kinds of sequoias: the giant sequoia and the evergreen sequoia. The largest of the giant sequoias is General Sherman. This tree is almost 4,000 years old and stands 83 metres high with a diameter at the base of 10 metres. There are specimens that are higher but have less bulk than the General Sherman tree.

Evergreen sequoias do not live as long as the giant variety but they grow taller. Founder's Tree, which is in California, is just over 110 metres high. The trunk of this tree is thinner and has a base diameter of about 5 metres.

Where chewing gum comes from

Some 90 per cent of the chewing gum produced in the United States comes from chicle, the solidified milky juice of the sapodilla tree. This is a tropical evergreen which grows to more than 15 metres in height and has many branches with glossy, light green leaves that are oval in shape. The trees grow wild in the forests of southern Mexico and northern central America.

The wood of the sapodilla is very hard and stands up well to

Original distribution of the Indian tribes

Dull Knife and his people head for home

bad weather. The Mayas, the ancient people who lived in Central America, used sapodilla wood for building, and many examples of this wood, still in good condition, have been found in Maya ruins.

The fruit of the sapodilla tree contains a jelly-like fluid. When this fluid hardens it turns into a pink gum that can be chewed. The material most used in making chewing gum is the latex, or milky fluid, that flows in the trunk of the tree. This latex is obtained by making deep V-shaped cuts in the bark of the tree; the juice runs down these cuts and is gathered in cups. The latex is taken from the tree during the rainy season when the sapodilla tree has the most juice.

Where to find the main Indian reservations

The merciless war between the white men and the Redskins in the American territories began in 1862 when Little Crow led his Sioux warriors in the massacre of 644 settlers in Minnesota. The Indians attacked the settlers because the Palefaces had taken away their prairie lands which they had used as hunting grounds.

The Indian wars lasted for about thirty years. They were very cruel and violent and ended in December 1890. The last battle in the wars was fought between the Sioux led by Big Foot and soldiers of the American army. From that day the Indians were made to live in special places called reservations which had strict limits and were more like prisons.

The map on the opposite page shows the location of the main Indian reservations. The largest is inhabited by the Navajo Indians who print their own newspaper dealing with Indian affairs. Despite difficulties in the early stages, most American Indians have now adapted themselves to the new way of life and live quite peacefully with the rest of the people of the United States. The 500,000 or so Indians who live in reservations have a democratic form of government, do a wide variety of jobs and have modern schools. Many Indians are taken for white people in the big cities.

Where to find poisonous snakes that are helpful to man

It seems incredible that there are snakes so poisonous that their bite is greatly feared and that at the same time these snakes should behave in such a way that they help man.

These are the coral snakes which live throughout America. They allow themselves to be picked up by people for they are very shy and tame and it is rare for anyone to be bitten by one. But it is not safe to play around with the coral snake: their poison is very powerful and can cause a swift death.

Coral snakes are shy only with people; with other snakes they are extremely aggressive. They eat many other reptiles, most of them poisonous, and in doing this, the coral snake destroys many poisonous creatures and clears large areas of reptiles which are dangerous to man.

Coral snakes have a brightly coloured skin marked with red, yellow and black rings. They live in sandy places where they bury themselves. When their victims come along the coral snake darts out from its hiding place and kills them.

Laughing falcon with coral snake

Two coral snakes

Where some of the earliest reptiles appeared

One of the groups of animals from which the dinosaurs were descended was probably the *Seymouria*. The first fossilized remains of this animal were found in the lower Permian, a layer of rocks that dates back about 270 million years, in the red earth of Texas, near old pools of water.

The *Seymouria* was a small reptile whose remains have almost always been found in little hollows or crevices. For this reason some scientists believe the *Seymouria* lived in holes which it dug out by the sides of lakes and rivers. It is also possible that the bodies of these animals could have been dragged after their death into a crack that was already there. We know that the *Seymouria* moved very slowly along the ground, but in water it was an excellent swimmer.

An examination of their fossilized skeletons does not make it easy to see how the *Seymouria* breathed: they obviously had a very primitive respiratory system, consisting of swallowing air which was then pushed into the lungs through the movement of the ribs that covered the thorax, or chest.

Seymouria must have been very common because their fossilized remains have been found also in Bohemia, Czechoslovakia, and in Kazakhstan in the Soviet Union. It was a species of animal that soon died out.

Where the big cattle trails crossed the American prairies

At the end of the American Civil War in 1865 it has been estimated that there were 5 million head of cattle in the rich grasslands of Texas. There were so many cattle that they were worth only five dollars each as compared with forty dollars in the northern states. Because they wanted better prices for their animals, the Texan cattlemen decided to send their livestock to the growing industrial centres like Chicago and other cities in the north. But to reach the Kansas-Pacific Railway which transported the animals to their destination, the cattle had to be taken for hundreds of kilometres on exhausting journeys across territory that lurked with danger from hostile Indians, bandits and bad weather.

Huge herds of up to 4,000 cattle would be driven along the prairie trails amid great clouds of dust by tough cowboys. The main cattle centres were in Abilene on the Chisholm trail, Dodge City on the Western trail and Denver on the Goodnight-Loving trail.

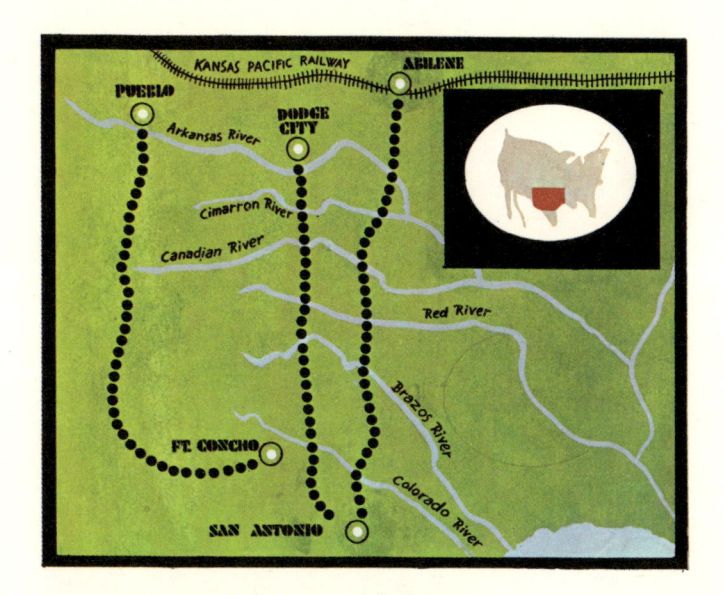

Sometimes the herds would be taken to the distant grasslands of the state of Dakota, the cowboys and cattle travelling for months at a time. When they arrived in the towns and received their wages the cowboys would have a wild time, drink vast quantities of whisky and get into fights and all sorts of trouble. When they had spent all their money the cowboys would go back to the ranch and their normal working life.

Where the first fossilized remains of the horned dinosaur were found

The first fossil remains of the *Triceratops*, also known as the horned dinosaur, were found in 1887 in Colorado.

These dinosaurs were about 6 metres long with an enormous skull that measured more than 2 metres. The skull was protected by a thick horny plate which had three big spikes or horns. The *Styracosaurus* was about the same size as the *Triceratops*, but it looked even more terrifying because of the enormous crest on top of its bony skull.

When the first extraordinary remains were found in Colorado the study dealing with ancient forms of life, palaeontology, was still in its early stages. It had just begun to study the great reptiles which existed over 135 million years ago during the Mesozoic Era of the Earth's history. Scientists in 1887 believed that all dinosaurs looked alike and for this reason they did not think that the enormous skull they had found belonged to a reptile. They believed instead it was the skull of a very ancient form of mammal and they gave this animal the scientific name of *bisons alticornis*. But two years later the scientists came across the skeletons of dinosaurs which had been preserved in a better state. These skeletons belonged to a kind of dinosaur which had been completely unknown before, a dinosaur with thick armour-plating which must have made it look like a living tank.

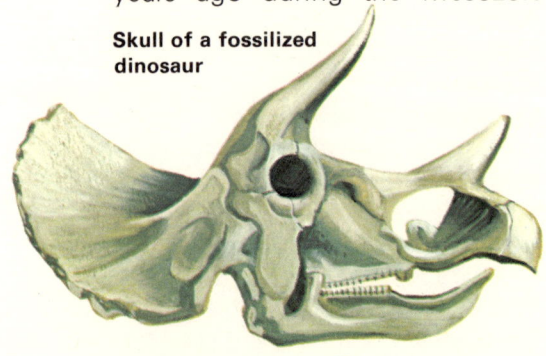

There are many fossil remains in Colorado and Utah. In Utah there are so many remains of these huge animals that an entire area of the state has been turned into an open-air museum.

Skull of a fossilized dinosaur

(Triceratops)

Where the giant cactus grows

In dry, tropical regions there are plants of the succulent family that grow to gigantic sizes. In Europe, under the best conditions, cactus plants rarely grow to more than one metre high, but in deserts such plants are as tall as trees and have huge, straight branches.

The giant cactus of the Arizona desert in the United States is the largest type of cactus. It can grow to 15 metres tall and weigh as much as 4 tons. It is easy to imagine how much water this plant can store in its thick, ribbed trunk which is like a green fluted column. Some desert birds such as the owl and the woodpecker make their nests in its vertical branches.

The giant cactus has a life span of more than 200 years.

Where the burrowing owl lives

The ways of owls are much the same the world over. But there is one owl, a native of America, which is very unusual because it is quite unique in the bird kingdom. This is the burrowing owl. It has this name because instead of building the usual rough nest in a sheltered gorge, the burrowing owl prefers to live in the home of a digging animal such as the anteater, the armadillo or the prairie dog.

The owl does not take over a burrow that has been abandoned by its owner but frequently shares one, living quite peacefully together with the real owner of the burrow. Unlike other owls, the burrowing owl goes hunting by day. It stands perfectly still and waits for its victim to come close, rather than fly after it.

Where to find the main space control centre of the United States

The space control centre at Houston, Texas, is the best-known of the centres set up by NASA (National Aeronautics and Space Administration). These centres were designed to help in the great adventure of exploring the Moon. All the instructions to the astronauts on the Moon were sent from Houston. It was the Houston space centre which received all the data about the performance of the lunar landing craft, known as the LM (lunar module), about the health of the astronauts and about the valuable information which these highly skilled men sent back to the Earth as they worked on the Moon.

Strangely enough this famous space centre is not situated at Cape Canaveral (called Cape Kennedy from 1963–73) where all the great Moon rockets have been launched. Houston is in Texas, about 1,500 kilometres west of Florida. The NASA space centre is located a few kilometres southeast of Houston and has the most advanced forms of electronic control equipment. It also receives technical information sent by seventeen monitoring stations throughout the world. The information is immediately turned into computer code. An army of technicians keeps a close watch on the various screens making it almost impossible for a mistake to be made in guiding the space flight from Earth. With the Apollo Moon landings now completed, the Houston space centre is at present engaged on even more important tasks in space.

The English fort at New York

Where the first inhabited centre of New York arose

New York City is the most important and heavily populated city of the United States and is also one of the oldest. New York Bay was discovered in 1524 by the Italian explorer Giovanni da Verrazano, but it was the Dutch who first lived in what is now the city of New York, calling their first settlement New Amsterdam. This settlement was on Manhattan Island which the Dutch bought from local Indians for a ridiculously small amount. The city soon prospered and people from many countries went to live there.

In 1664 an English naval fleet of warships sailed into the harbour. The settlers did not want to put up any resistance and the whole city passed under British control without a shot being fired.

From that day New Amsterdam became known as New York after the Duke of York who became King James II of England.

Today New York City with its suburbs has a population of more than 12 million inhabitants. The city occupies an area of 744 square kilometres, its greatest length from north to south is 58 kilometres and it is 16 kilometres wide. It occupies the whole estuary of the Hudson River.

Where sisal is produced

Sisal is a very tough fibre obtained from the large, fleshy leaves of the agave plant that is grown mainly in eastern Africa and Mexico. It takes from two to seven years for the plant to be ready to produce sisal. The agave's leaves are cut every year but they keep growing again until the plant dies. The fibre is obtained by crushing the leaves to get rid of their juicy pulp and then washing them in running water. Sisal is used to make coarse textiles, rope and string.

Where to find the most famous geyser in America

In the famous Yellowstone National Park of the United States there are some 200 active geysers, two of which come into action and spout with impressive regularity. One of these geysers is called the Five-Minute Man; the other is named Old Faithful. The first geyser is rather small: it shoots up a column of boiling water every five minutes. Old Faithful is larger, rising with a roar to the sky every 65 minutes, its column of water exceeding 40 metres. This geyser keeps spouting for about five minutes at a time.

Geysers make an impressive sight. They usually rise from a fairly small hole in the ground surrounded by rock. When they rise they make a loud roaring, rumbling sound and send a jet of boiling water shooting upwards. As the geyser spouts the dull noise of thunder can be heard for up to many hundreds of metres. The height of the column of water varies from centimetres to more than 100 metres according to the geyser.

Where to find the glass palace of the United Nations

The United Nations consists of an association of nations whose governments are pledged to maintain peace and international security and to promote friendly relations among countries.

The United Nations was formed on 24 October 1945, in New York City. It consists of a General Assembly of all the member states which meets regularly every year; a Security Council; an Economic and Social Council; a Trusteeship Council; the International Court of Justice; and the Secretariat.

All these organs have their seat of power in New York City, except for the International Court of Justice which is at The Hague in the Netherlands.

The tall Secretariat building is situated between the East River and First Avenue. It has thirty-nine floors, stands just over 166 metres, is 88 metres long and about 22 metres wide.

Where America's biggest river flows

The Mississippi is about 3,760 kilometres long. With its two huge tributaries, the Missouri and the Ohio, it drains a vast area, emptying the water from thirty-one states and two Canadian provinces into the Gulf of Mexico.

The enormous delta of the Mississippi starts in Louisiana, about 400 kilometres from the sea. At this place an arm of the river flows away from the main course and becomes the river Atchafalaya. Beyond this point the Mississippi opens out like a fan and develops several mouths when it reaches the sea.

The Mississippi divides the United States into two clear-cut regions. In the east lie the well-watered lands which were once covered in forests but are now intensively farmed; in the west lie the prairies which are bordered by dry, desert regions, on the slopes of the Rocky Mountains.

Up to the point where it meets the Ohio River, the Mississippi follows a steep downward course and flows between rocky banks. Once it has reached the flat land of the plains, it meanders and flows very slowly. Often the surrounding land is lower than the river itself and at these places strong ramparts and flood barriers have been built, but it has not always been possible to escape the disastrous floods that happen when the river bursts its banks. Large boats can sail up the Mississippi as far as New Orleans which is about 160 kilometres from the delta; smaller ships can go as far as Baton Rouge.

The Mississippi was discovered by Hernando de Soto in May 1541. Its source, however, remained a mystery until 1832 when Henry Rowe Schodcraft found it in a small lake in Minnesota, which he named Itasca from the Latin *veritas caput* (true head).

Where alligators live

The reptiles of American rivers are different from true crocodiles. The main dissimilarity is in the shape of the face, for the alligator has broader and shorter jaws. It is also smaller than a crocodile, growing up to 4 metres in length, and the bony plates on its body are arranged in a different manner. Caymans, as some alligators are called, belong to central and southern America, but alligators live mainly along the Mississippi and its tributaries. At one time there were a large number of alligators, but many were killed by hunters for their valuable skins.

An alligator's life is rather like that of a crocodile. Alligators love to sleep for hours in the sun, stretched out on the river bank. Sometimes they float motionless on the water and look like logs of wood drifting in the current, but if any animal dares to venture into the water, the alligator will drag it to the bottom and tear it to pieces. The alligator does not eat its victim straight away: instead it leaves the meat until it is more tender.

Prop roots of the swamp cypress, (*Taxodium distichum*) and (right) the proproots of the *Iriartea*.

De Soto sees the Mississippi for the first time

Where the swamp cypress grows

The swamp or bald cypress (*Taxodium distichum*) is also known as the Virginia cypress because it grows in great numbers in the marshy regions of that state. Its chief characteristic is its roots which form large lumps sometimes a metre high, sticking out of the water all round the tree. The trunk of the swamp cypress is straight and grows to as high as 40 metres, with a diameter of 5 metres or more at the base.

The swamp cypress is very common in the marshes of Florida, where it forms small dense forests scattered over the region. Many swamp cypresses also grow in woods near rivers forming part of the Mississippi delta and in the lower Rio Grande valley, Mexico.

Where the magnolia trees come from

There are about eighty species of magnolia: about fifty of these come from Asian countries such as Japan and Java and the rest are natives of North America. In Louisiana this tree forms entire forests and its beautiful blossoms have been chosen as the emblem of the state.

The magnolia became popular in Europe for its elegant appearance and decorative effect. The most common of the American varieties is the *magnolia grandiflora* which has very large and striking flowers. The magnolia is a tall tree and grows to more than 25 metres high. Its branches are a rust-red colour, covered in tiny little hairs, and the bark of the tree is blackish and wrinkled. The fruits are pear-shaped and contain seeds of a beautiful coral-red which are seen when these fruits are ripe.

Where to find the national park of the Everglades

The Florida peninsula in the south of the United States is not only famous for Cape Canaveral, but also for its climate and its own special type of plant life. The famous Everglades swamps were once a paradise for hunters but today 3,484 square kilometres of the Everglades have been turned into a national park.

The dense forests of the Everglades contain wonderful examples of tropical plants and swamp vegetation. In this setting there lives a host of unusual animals: reptiles, including large alligators and snakes that are very poisonous; land animals like the cougar, bobcat and opposum; and, especially, a large number of birds such as the egret and spoonbill. Many animals that were typical of the Everglades were wiped out by hunters, but the remaining examples now live under the protection of laws which forbid almost every form of hunting in the area.

In the more remote part of the Everglades there still live the last descendants of the Indian Semi-

Seminole Indians

nole tribe. The Seminole resistance to giving up their lands resulted in wars (between 1817 and 1858) and the removal of most of the tribe to Indian Territory (later Oklahoma). By the 1960s there were about 3,000 Seminoles in Oklahoma and 1,000 in southern Florida.

Where to find the Cape Canaveral launching pad

The world's most famous rocket-launching pad is certainly that of Cape Canaveral, which for ten years, 1963–73, was called Cape Kennedy. It was from here that the Saturn rockets were sent into space on their journey to the Moon.

Cape Canaveral is situated on a small peninsula on the eastern coast of Florida, facing the Atlantic Ocean. By a strange coincidence, Jules Verne launched his imaginary rockets to the Moon from Florida. Cape Canaveral includes gigantic fixed installations as well as the launching mechanisms that have been built there.

The operations rooms are inside a four-storey block. In these rooms there are 450 control panels which tell the technicians everything they need to know about the countdown. There are also sixty television screens which give a picture of every part of the rocket that is about to be launched.

The largest building is the VAB (Vehicle Assembly Building). It is inside this building that the various rocket stages of the Saturn are put together. The huge gantries that support the rocket on the pad and the emergency escapes are also assembled in the VAB.

A canal joins the VAB with the Atlantic Ocean. Barges sail along this canal to deliver the various stages of the Saturn rocket.

The lift-off of an Apollo mission to the Moon (left)

The astronaut Michael Collins (below)

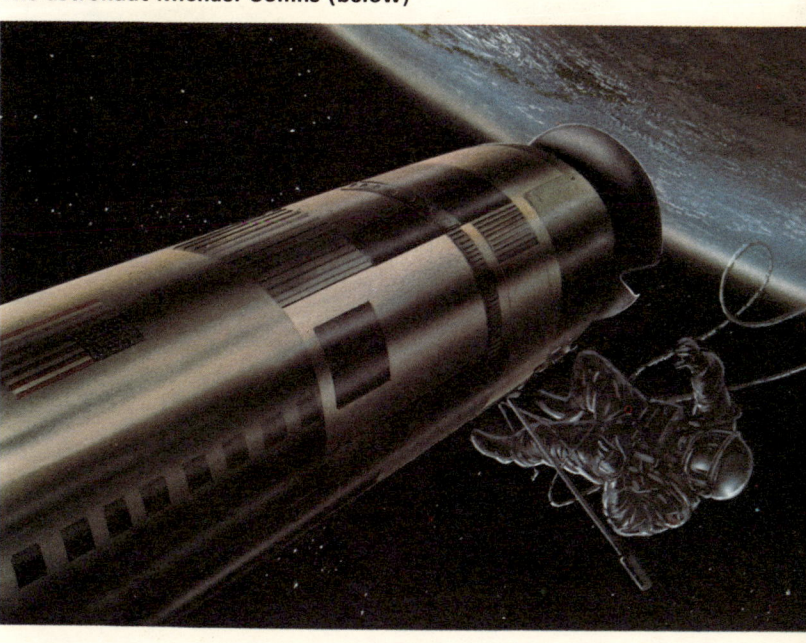

Where bison live

The bison are typical ruminants of the great prairies of North America where they are commonly called buffalo. When the first settlers went to the west there were an estimated 60 million of these animals who provided the Indians with their major source of food and skins; but the Indians only killed when necessary.

Then the white man came and the massacre began. During the years across the continent, these animals were wantonly slaughtered by the hundreds of thousands. The white settlers only used the tongue of the bison and the animal's bones were sold by the ton for a few dollars to be made into fertilizer.

Finally all but a few bison were killed. Today they are carefully protected and are breeding again in great numbers.

Where the main battles between the Indians and the whites took place

The massacre of the bison by the whites was one of the causes of Indian anger that led these nomads of the prairie to declare a merciless war.

Those responsible for the extermination of the Indians knew very well that the only way to crush Indian resistance was to deprive them of their bison, their main source of food. These white men, led by Phil Sheridan, went hunting the bison: even the American army encouraged this activity. For several years bands of hunters went through the prairie, leaving behind them a land strewn with the carcases of thousands of dead animals. The famous Buffalo Bill alone killed 4,280 bison in seventeen months.

At the end of this mad hunt

Skirmish between soldiers and the Sioux

more than 50 million bison had been killed. In the meantime the hatred of the Indians had been roused. Indian attacks on the whites which had previously been sporadic, now increased. From east to west ran the word: 'Death to the white man'.

The first of the cruel massacres of this unequal war between the two peoples took place in 1862 in Minnesota when Little Crow led his Sioux warriors in a massacre of 644 settlers. Many other massacres followed in various parts of the west. One well known one was the killing of eighty men led by Captain Fetterman who had come from Fort Kearny in Wyoming some time earlier at Christmas 1866. Perhaps the most famous was the massacre on 25 June 1876 of 300 cavalrymen under the command of General Custer at Little Bighorn in Montana by 4,000 Indians led by Chief Sitting Bull.

But these episodes which enraged the whites and stirred them to revenge, were only a reply, often a weak reply, to the very cruel massacres which the settlers and soldiers carried out in Indian villages. These villages were almost always defenceless and populated by old men, women and and children. The stories of the time often failed to mention the damage that was being done against the Indians in order to stress the cruelty that was suffered by the whites.

Apart from the individual episodes the words of Chief Red Cloud uttered to the white leaders remain true: 'When you first came to this land you were few and we were many. Now we are few. . . . In other days our people possessed vast areas of land, today we have no more than an island.'

The last conflict between the Sioux and the American army took place at Pine Ridge on 29 December 1890 when soldiers of the U.S. Seventh Cavalry massacred by gunfire more than 200 Indians in a village, most of them women and children. A few days earlier Chief Sitting Bull, who had been taken prisoner by the army, had been killed.

Where the first inhabitants of America came from

According to the latest studies the first human beings appear to have come to America about 20,000 years ago. This was during one of the great Ice Ages that affected the Earth during the Quaternary Era of its history. At that time enormous glaciers joined Asia and North America, forming a natural bridge between the two continents across the Bering Strait. It was over this bridge that waves of Asiatic people of Mongoloid stock passed, pushing on farther to the south as time went on.

Little by little these peoples grew accustomed to their new surroundings and their descendants completed the occupation of the entire American continent, reaching its southernmost tip at what is now Tierra del Fuego. The descendants of those ancient peoples still live in that region.

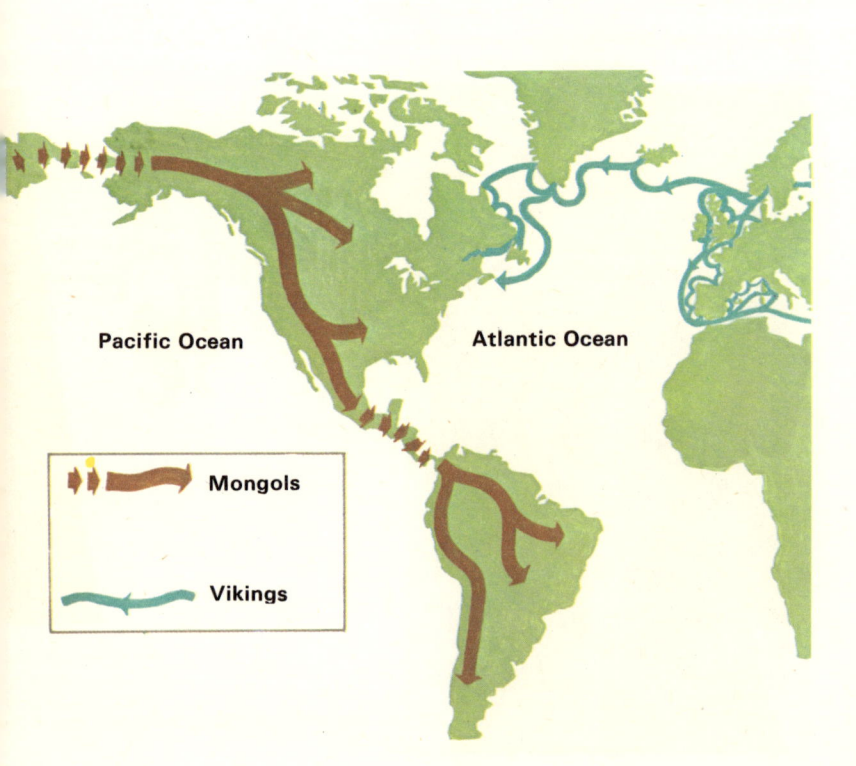

Where gold fever broke out in the Wild West

The gold rush in America began on the day when a certain James Marshall discovered the first nuggets quite by chance in the waters of the river Sacramento. It was 24 January 1848. The news that California had major gold deposits soon spread far and wide. The gold rush turned into a frantic stampede towards the region of the river Sacramento by gold prospectors and adventurers. Those who did not want to waste time on the long sea journey by way of Cape Horn (the Panama Canal had not yet been opened), faced the terrible hardships of the Oregon trail, crossing the Sierra Nevada mountains and coping with all the difficulties of such a journey. Nevertheless tens of thousands of people went to the west, lured on by dreams of riches.

In 1848 California had 22,000 inhabitants. Ten years later this figure had grown to 225,000. Some of the prospectors became rich but others were bitterly disappointed. Later gold was also discovered in Colorado, Nevada, Montana and in the Yukon.

Where to find the siren

The siren is an amphibious animal and not to be confused with the mythological creatures of the same name. In the myths, sirens sang sweet songs to lure ships and their sailors to destruction on dangerous rocks; but the siren dealt with here is an ugly creature and a close relative of the proteus which is a cave-dwelling amphibian of Europe.

The Sirenidae family of animals always live in marshy regions of North America. They belong to a group of animals about which little is yet known.

The great siren is the largest of the species. It is about 90 centimetres long and makes its home in the swamps where it constantly rummages through the mud in search of insects, grubs and molluscs. The great siren also eats small fish which it catches by skilful swimming.

Where the first Europeans landed in America

Europeans first landed in North America as early as A.D. 1000, but for many years afterwards nobody in Europe knew about the expeditions of Vikings led by Leif Ericsson. It took another 500 years until Christopher Columbus discovered America by accident. For a long time after its discovery America remained a vast continent to be conquered and stripped of its riches.

The first settlement of Europeans who sailed to the continent with the intention of making it their home was founded at Jamestown in Virginia by English settlers in 1607. A previous attempt in 1587 had ended in disaster. But the date of the real beginning of colonization in America is 21 November 1620 when 102 Pilgrim Fathers landed at Cape Cod from their ship the *Mayflower*.

Led by William Bradford the Pilgrim Fathers soon built up a flourishing colony. Shortly afterwards other Europeans came to America. Their life in the early settlements was hard, with the constant threat of attack by hostile Indians. They also faced the danger of famine and disease but gradually the colonists overcame their difficulties and became the true masters of the new world.

The *Mayflower*

Indians attacking a farm

Where the pioneer trails to the west were made

The date of the start of the conquest of the west by the American pioneers can be fixed at 1843. It was in this year that thousands of families set out for the territory of Oregon, urged on by the preaching of the missionary Marcus Whitman who told them about all the wonders of the new promised lands.

The move to the west attracted growing numbers of people in the years that followed. In 1850 alone at Fort Laramie, which was one of the stopping points on the journey, there were 37,750 men, 825 women and 1,126 children. The journey west was full of all kinds of danger. The pioneers travelled in covered wagons, pulled by oxen, inside which were their household goods, farm tools, seeds and all their worldly belongings.

The Oregon trail passed through the prairies and climbed up the mountains for more than 3,200 kilometres until it reached the river Columbia. At that point the pioneers continued their journey on rafts. There were three main trails that began at Missouri River and led to the lands of the west: the Oregon trail, the California trail and the Santa Fe trail. Many thousands of pioneers died and were buried along these trails, the victims of storms, mud, disease and the attacks by wild Indians. Those who lived through these dangers were sustained by their courage until they reached their promised land in the west that was to reward all their hopes. During those years the pioneers laid the foundations of new and important cities in America.

Where the trail of the legendary Pony Express ran

By 1860 there were many large cities and towns established by the settlers in the American west. These towns needed a form of rapid communication with the rich cities of the east where practically all of America's industry and trade had its headquarters. In 1858 the stage-coaches of John Butterfield operated a weekly service between the civilized east and the wild west. The stagecoach services were quite regular in spite of attacks by Indians and bandits.

But a quicker form of communication was needed and in 1860 the Pony Express service came into being, making it possible to deliver mail quickly between the east and California. The riders who carried out this service were picked from the finest and bravest men of the west. A Pony Express rider had to cover a distance of 125 kilometres a day, changing horses in a few seconds and carrying a satchel containing 10 kilogrammes of mail.

From St Joseph in Missouri the trail of the Pony Express went across savage territories for 2,944 kilometres as far as Sacramento in California. It passed through Fort Kearney, Fort Laramie, Fort Bridger, Salt Lake City and Carson City. The entire journey took nine days but the record was seven days seven hours. When the first telegraph service was opened the Pony Express came to an end.

Where the Pacific Railroad began

With the arrival of hundreds of thousands of settlers in the American west, many cities and towns had sprung up. It became necessary to have some means of carrying the large amounts of farm produce as quickly as possible from the lands of the west to the rich cities on the Atlantic coast, and return with the goods manufactured by the growing industries of the United States.

On 10 June 1861, President Abraham Lincoln signed a decree for the construction of the Pacific Railroad. Two large companies, the Union Pacific and the Central Pacific, started work at the same time from opposite ends of the planned route. On 10 May 1869, after many difficulties, the two lines were joined together at Promontory Point in Utah.

A rider of the Pony Express

The Union Pacific and the Central Pacific met in Utah in 1869

Objects dating from before Columbus' arrival in America

In Central and South America from about 2000 B.C. there are traces of several villages and places of worship. The oldest of these are situated in the mountains of Peru, but there are others in Mexico too. This region appears to have been the cradle of America's major civilizations. It was here that the civilization and culture of the Toltecs, among others, was born. The Toltec civilization was probably the most important in ancient America and influenced the later civilizations of the Aztecs and the Mayas. The Toltecs' main centre was at Tula, a city-state that was the seat of a great dynasty of kings.

Where to find the legendary Fort Alamo

Fort Alamo, the scene of a terrible massacre in which the famous Davy Crockett was killed, is in Texas where the city of San Antonio now stands. Texas was a Mexican colony which Americans began to infiltrate from 1820. In 1836 there were so many of these Americans and they had become so powerful that they demanded independence from Mexico. They defied the troops of the Mexican army but at the Alamo, behind the stockade of an old Spanish mission, about 187 of them were trapped and besieged by the army of General de Santa Anna. The bravery of the fort's defenders could only stand up to the enemy for two weeks and on 6 March 1836 Santa Anna led his troops in a final attack, killing everyone in the fort. Some weeks later, however, the Mexicans were defeated by the colonists at San Jacinto and the Texans won their independence.

Where to find America's most ancient human settlements

We know that the first inhabitants of the Americas were of Asian origin. These people crossed the Bering Strait about 20,000 years ago and followed the frozen trails of Alaska, moving gradually southwards. It would therefore seem reasonable to believe that America's longest-inhabited places were in the north. In this region the ancient Americans would have established their settlements before sending advance parties farther south.

Archaeological excavations, however, prove that the oldest inhabited centres first arose in Central and South America. There must have been some early settlements in the north but little trace of these has been found.

Where Columbus landed

When Columbus finally sighted land on 12 October 1492, after a voyage of more than two months, he was convinced that he had reached India. He was so sure that the first savages he met after going on land he called Indians.

We now know that on his first voyage Columbus did not even touch the American continent but merely explored some of the islands of the Bahamas. One of these was San Salvador which Columbus named in Spanish after the Holy Saviour, Jesus Christ, in gratitude for the success of his journey.

Before returning to Europe, Columbus reached the shores of Cuba. He was still sure he was in India but he was disappointed that he found no gold or spices. At last, on 5 December 1492, Columbus landed at Hispaniola, which today is divided into the two countries of Haiti and the Dominican Republic. On this island he left a garrison of Spanish volunteers to take charge of the new lands.

Columbus landing at Hispaniola in 1492

Where the ring-tail cat lives

In the regions of Central America, in certain parts of the United States and especially in Mexico, the ring-tail cat is a very common animal. In Mexico City it is kept as a household pet like an ordinary domestic cat, although the ring-tail cat is not easily domesticated.

The most striking feature of this small mammal is its long, bushy tail marked with black and white rings which give this cat a very individual appearance. The ring-tail cat's body fur is greyish-brown, thick and soft, with white patches over the eyes. It has long ears and a pointed snout and its voice is a bark. This animal is the American equivalent of the European pole-cats and martens.

The ring-tail cat is an excellent climber and often lives in trees where it catches birds, small mammals and other little creatures on which it feeds. Sometimes it lives in deserts. It spends the day in well-sheltered lairs and comes out at night.

Pueblo Indians

Where the civilization of the ancient American Pueblo Indians flourished

The Pueblo were a people who lived in villages in North America. Before the Spanish conquest they were spread over a vast territory which included southern California, northern Mexico and the land to the east as far as Texas. The descendants of these people still live in scattered, poor villages known as pueblos. Today these places have none of their past splendour.

In parts of Colorado there are the remains of ancient pueblos which reached their greatest development about 1300. Perhaps the most beautiful of these is Pueblo Bonito in the valley of the Rio San Juan. This village is shaped like an amphitheatre in which the houses rise like steps one above the other.

Pueblo houses were built of bricks made from compressed and dried mud and sometimes consisted of up to four storeys. They were often built in stepped-back style, so that the strongly built flat roofs of the lower rooms formed terraces for the rooms above and provided the only means of access.

Where the cashew grows

The *acaju*, or cashew, is a native plant of tropical America but today it is cultivated in most warm countries for its excellent nuts. The tree grows on ground that is lower than 800 metres and needs a warm, moist climate. The fruit, which is particularly popular in

Brazil where it ripens between November and January, is quite odd-looking. It resembles a large pear as big as a man's fist, at the bottom of which is a woody growth shaped like a kidney.

In actual fact the real fruit is this curved nut at the bottom of the fruit. The most striking part of the fruit is the pear-shaped part which is really the greatly swollen stalk of the tree's blossom. This stalk becomes fleshy and rich in sugar substances.

Where to find Death Valley

The American pioneers gave this grim name of Death Valley to a very deep depression in Inyo, California, which at its bottom lies 85 metres below sea level. The entire valley had to be crossed by the prospectors in search of the famous gold deposits of California and many of these men lost their lives in Death Valley, dying of exhaustion and thirst. The pools of water that form in certain parts of the valley's floor are extremely salty, the climate is torrid and not one blade of grass grows there. It is a real hell-on-earth and the gold prospectors struggled to get through it, but often it was the end of their hopes.

In the 1870s when gold was discovered in the nearby mountains, thousands of skeletons of dead animals left behind by the pioneers marked the Death Valley trail. Hundreds of carcases littered the route and the ground was covered with wooden crosses on the graves of those people who had paid with their lives for the attempt to pass through its desolate wastes.

Where the Mayas lived

The region where the Maya civilization developed forms part of what is now Yucatan, Guatemala and Honduras. It is a broad area that lies between the Atlantic and Pacific Oceans, with a tropical climate and where abundant rainfall has created large and flourishing forests. The territory is crossed by a chain of mountains which are volcanic in origin.

The Mayas first came to this land before the birth of Christ. For a long time they lived a primitive form of life but towards A.D. 300 their civilization began to develop. The Mayas had a different appearance from other inhabitants of the region: they were round-headed and usually not very tall. They lived in city-states and kept alive their awareness of being one race.

The largest Maya city, founded in 416 and named Tikal, included five groups of great buildings which were joined by elevated roadways. This city had eight gigantic pyramids more than 70 metres high, the ruins of which still give us an idea of their ancient splendour.

Guatemalan costumes

Where *philodendrons* come from

Philodendron is the name given to about 200 species of plants, many of which are popular houseplants in Europe. They come from tropical America and are liked for the gloss, variegation and colour of their leaves. The name *philodendron* is from the Greek meaning 'lover of trees', for most *philodendrons* are like vines, living in the shade of tall trees and clinging closely to them. It is this liking for shade that has made the *philodendrons* ideal for growing in enclosed places such as houses and flats.

One of the most popular *philodendrons* is the *Monstera deliciosa*, a native of Mexico, whose large, perforated leaves appear to be cut full of holes. Along the main trunk of the plant, at the base of the stem of each leaf, there appears a greyish-brown knob which grows longer and longer as the plant grows older. These knobs are roots and in the forests they grow to the ground or into cracks in the bark of trees where they both support and feed the plant.

Where liquidambar for perfume is produced

One of the first 'unknown' trees about which news was brought to Europe by the explorers who had travelled to America, was the liquidambar. The tree has this name because it contains a liquid resin, storax, which is extracted by cutting the bark of the tree. The wood of the liquidambar tree is used in medicine and perfumes.

Liquidambar trees vary in height from 10 to 45 metres. The liquid extracted from the trunk is sweet-smelling but bitter to the taste, and is made into chewing gum after being processed.

The first man to find this perfumed resin was Fernando Cortés. In 1519 he met for the first time Montezuma, Emperor of the Aztecs. During the ceremonies, resin was burned inside small golden urns. The Aztecs also used to smoke the leaves of the liquidambar tree and mixed them with tobacco leaves.

The University of Mexico

Where to find the huge dams of Tennessee

The Tennessee River is the largest tributary of the Ohio River and the Ohio, in its turn, flows into the Mississippi. The Tennessee River Valley used to suffer from disastrous floods almost every year, caused by the rushing waters of the river swollen by the heavy rains of the wet season. The Tennessee Valley Authority was set up in 1933 by the U.S. government, to control these floods, improve navigation and produce electric power.

Today thirty-two dams with six huge reservoirs prevent flooding and make it possible for vast areas to be irrigated. Huge electric power stations use the force of the water to produce a generating capacity of nearly 12 million kilowatts.

Where the capital of the Aztecs was situated

The history of the Aztecs starts at the beginning of the twelfth century A.D. when these people invaded the central plateau of Mexico from the north. They settled in a marshy zone that was rich in reeds and willows. The Toltecs who had lived in Mexico for 2,000 years and had built up a great civilization, regarded the Aztecs as barbarians just like any other breed of warriors and hunters. Such barbarians had come to the land before and had interbred with the natives.

The Aztecs, who were also known as the Mexica (the country was named after them), did not know how to cultivate the soil or how to weave material for cloth and they lived in miserable little huts. But they regarded themselves as a chosen people, believing that with the help of their god, Huitzilopochtli, they were destined to conquer the whole world. It was this god, according to the legend, who told the ancient Aztec leaders where their capital city was to be built. This was to be where an eagle, clutching a snake in its talons, would come to rest on a cactus to eat its prey. So, on such a spot, a temple was built on a small rocky island in Lake Texcoco. This temple was the first beginning of the city of Tenochtitlan, which became the capital of this proud people. The city grew rapidly and in less than 200 years it became a splendid place. The Aztecs assimilated the culture of the native people and proved to be great architects, building on a series of islets a row of magnificent palaces connected by bridges, elevated roadways and terraces. According to the chronicles of the time, the city resembled Venice, with more than a million inhabitants, 50,000 houses, fine temples and imperial palaces. After the Spaniards came this great city was razed to the ground.

The temple at Tenochtitlan

Ancient map of Mexico City

107

THE WHERE OF SOUTH AMERICA

Where to find the world's largest forest

The world's largest forest covers the vast river basins of the Amazon and the Orinoco. The enormous growth of vegetation in this zone is due to its proximity to the equator. It is extremely warm and the air is very humid because of the heavy rainfall that can last from six to eight months.

The sub-equatorial forest is dense and impenetrable with many layers of vegetation, each growing to a different height. Flying over such a forest in an aeroplane one can only see the tops of the highest trees which, massed together, give the impression of an immense sea of green from which only those trees with very tall trunks emerge to heights of more than 40 metres.

Underneath this top layer grow tree ferns and beneath them are shrubs, grasses and climbing plants known as *lianas*. Human beings or large animals can only go through such forests by following the almost invisible tracks made by animals going to their water-holes.

South American fuschia

Where the first fuchsia plants were found

The dense forests of South America are the native places of the fuchsia, those beautiful flowering plants that can be kept in a pot or grown in gardens. There are many species of fuchsia which vary considerably in size and other characteristics.

The fuchsia were used to the dark atmosphere of dense forests and when the first plants were brought to Europe they did not stand up well to strong sunlight. Later, as hybrid forms of the plant were produced, stronger specimens began to grow and flourish in almost every kind of climate. The many varieties of fuchsia are quite easy to grow and are very resistant to many plant diseases. In winter, however, they should be kept in a greenhouse.

Usually the brightly coloured flowers in shades of red, blue, purple and white, droop down from the branches, but there are also fuchsias which have flowers that stand up straight and the plant is as big as a small tree.

Where to find the world's highest railways

In Peru the trains climb up the Andes mountains to a height of 4,816 metres. This is the railway line that starts at Callao on the Pacific coast and goes to La Oroya: it is the highest railway line in the world.

The railway line from Rio Mulato to Potosi reaches a height of just over 4,787 metres, almost as high as Mont Blanc, Europe's tallest mountain. The highest railway line in Europe is at the Jungfrau in Switzerland and reaches a height of just over 3,454 metres.

On these South American lines the trains set out at sea level and reach great heights so rapidly that nurses travel on them to help the passengers with oxygen masks if they feel ill as a result of the rapid change in air pressure and the thinness of the air. The railways across the Andes provide vital links between the lowland regions, but the cost of construction and maintenance is very great.

Trains climb the mountains to a height of 4,816 metres

Bolivian girl

Where to find the world's highest capital city

At the foot of the soaring peaks of Mount Illampu (6,550 metres) and Mount Illimani (6,459 metres) on the Andes mountain range, stands the city of La Paz, the capital of Bolivia, founded by the Spaniards in 1548.

Situated on a high plateau a little south of Lake Titicaca, this city of almost 400,000 inhabitants rises to a height of 3,658 metres, the highest capital city in the world. But it is not the world's highest city. Oruro, for example, which has almost 100,000 inhabitants, is 3,715 metres above sea level. There are even higher inhabited places: the village of Chacaltaya, lost in the mountains of the Andes, is 5,130 metres above sea level which is higher than the summit of Mont Blanc.

At such altitudes the air is very thin and contains less oxygen, but the Indians can live and work in these conditions without suffering too much. For thousands of years they have been used to living at great altitudes and their bodies have become adapted to the severe climate of the Andes. As a result of breathing in the thin air they have developed large chests to extract as much oxygen as possible from the air.

Bolivia has no sea coast and its territory is almost completely covered by mountains. These include high mountain chains in the west and a number of high plateaux, most of them arid and all of them about 4,000 metres above sea level. In the east the land slopes gently away downwards to the immense river basin of the Amazon.

Where the world's most famous carnival takes place

Washed by three waters of Guanabara Bay and dominated by the Pão de Açucar (Sugarloaf Mountain), Rio de Janeiro is one of the most fascinating cities in the world. Discovered by the Portuguese in 1502, it was the capital of Brazil until 1960 when Brazilia became the new capital. Rio is a busy trading port, has flourishing industries and more than 4 million inhabitants. But what has made this city famous throughout the world is the carnival that takes place there every year.

In February of each year Rio turns into a huge and colourful stage for dancing and for decorated floats that parade past huge crowds from all over the world. For a whole month music and laughter reign supreme, but it is during the last three days that the festival reaches its climax, and there is non-stop dancing in the streets of Copacabana.

Chile monkey-puzzle tree

Where the monkey puzzle tree comes from

These strange trees are evergreen and their branches are covered in thousands of dark-green, scale-like leaves. They resemble the fossilized remains of very ancient trees that grew many millions of years ago. These are trees of the *Araucaria* family, conifers that first grew in Brazil and in the Andes mountains, and later became popular in Europe.

The best-known is the *Araucaria araucana*, the Chile pine or monkey puzzle tree which was introduced into Britain in 1796. In South America this tree grows as high as 50 metres. It has a blackish, wrinkled bark and the branches grow straight out from the trunk, separated into tiers. The leaves have no stems and are small and stiff with a spiky end. From a distance the tree looks as if it has green branches with no leaves and has a stiff, rigid appearance.

Where alpacas are reared

Recent archaeological excavations in the Andes where the oldest Indian civilizations once flourished, have discovered valuable remains of old woven cloth that dates back to about 4,000 years ago. These woven materials were made from the wool of the alpaca, an animal greatly valued by the ancient peoples of South America for its long, soft fur.

The alpaca is a typical animal of the Andes mountains. It is a close relative of the llama and, like the llama, is descended from the wild guanaco, which is still hunted in the mountains of Peru and Bolivia. The alpaca rather resembles a sheep, with a neck and face similar to a camel, but it is not a gentle animal like the sheep and is quite bad-tempered. Its wool grows to a length of more than 20 centimetres and is shorn every year.

Alpacas live in a semi-wild state on the slopes of the Andes

111

Where the terrible piranha fish lives

The natives of South America are terrified of the piranha fish, a fierce creature that resembles the tiger in its voracity. Piranha fish, which live in the rivers of South America, especially in the region of the Amazon and the Orinoco, can be included among the fiercest animals of the world.

Piranha fish are less than 40 centimetres long but they have massive jaws and strong razor-sharp teeth which are like a very sharp saw and can tear through even the toughest leather. The piranha's teeth are triangular in shape and fit exactly into one another; with such teeth these fish can tear even large animals to pieces.

Cattle are frequent victims of the piranha fish whenever they try to cross a river, but these fish will also attack human beings. When herdsmen want to take a herd of cattle across a river they select the worst beast and throw it into the water first. Attracted by the blood the piranha fish devour the animal while the rest of the herd is taken safely across the river.

Fierce piranha fish also attack human beings

Where to find the world's biggest estuary

The Amazon River is 6,280 kilometres long and the second-largest river in the world. It beats all world records for the amount of water it carries: every second it empties about 120,000 cubic metres of water into the ocean and when it is in flood this amount is almost doubled. At Manaus, which is about two-thirds of the way along the river's course, the Amazon is about 6 kilometres wide. At the estuary it broadens greatly to more than 200 kilometres. The waters of the Amazon penetrate so deeply into the Atlantic Ocean that at a distance of more than 300 kilometres from the coast one can still detect the presence of fresh water.

In 1500 Vicente Yáñez Pinzón discovered and explored the lower part of the Amazon and the following year the first descent from the Andes was made by Francisco de Orellana. But a complete survey of this river has still not been carried out, partly because of the hostility of the primitive Indian tribes who live in the dense virgin forest along the river's banks.

Where the guava comes from

The guava tree does not grow in Europe and its fruit is rarely seen in the shops. But in those parts of the world that have a tropical climate it is a common tree and it grows wild in some regions of Central America. It is not very tall and sometimes looks more like a large bush.

The tree is also known as the Indian pear because of the shape of its fruit which vary in size and weight. Guava fruit usually have a pinkish-white flesh but some are a reddish-purple, and they all have numerous small, hard seeds. Some varieties of guava smell of strawberries or raspberries.

The scent and the taste of guavas are always pleasant. These fruit are also a rich source of sugar and vitamin C, but they are very delicate and go bad quickly. For this reason they are rarely seen in Europe except as jellies and jams or in tins.

In some tropical countries the guava fruit is the basis of processing and canning industries. Guavas which are cultivated are produced from seeds. The tree takes several years to grow and mature but then it produces fruit for about twenty years.

Where arrowroot is produced

Pharmaceutical companies specializing in the manufacture of baby foods import large quantities of a light but nutritious flour known as arrowroot. This flour is obtained from the *Maranta arundinacea*, a beautiful herbaceous plant originally from the tropical regions of America. Today the arrowroot plant is also grown in India and parts of Africa.

The nutritive parts of the *Maranta* are found in the large underground roots or rhizomes. These have a high starch content, as well as some protein and salts, and are prepared in different ways as food by the natives of the region.

The *Maranta* also has another fine feature: a magnificent clump of shiny leaves that makes the plant very ornamental. This clump of leaves is a common feature in all the plants of this family which includes some 350 species.

Indians fishing in Rio Araguaia, Brazil

Cultivating land for agriculture

Marmoset

Where American monkeys live

Almost all the monkeys of the American continent live in the dense forests around the Amazon River. These monkeys spend most of their time in trees and are extremely agile acrobats, using their long tails to hang on to the branches. The best-known of these animals are the capuchin monkeys which were once the inseparable companions of travelling musicians and organ-grinders.

The capuchin monkeys are easily domesticated for they are gentle and good-natured and live well in captivity. For this reason there are always many of them in zoos and they are often sold in pet shops. They are not much bigger than a cat and are greyish-brown in colour with a long, hairy tail which is not so good at gripping things. They live mainly on fruit but also eat tender shoots and buds, insects and eggs which they steal from birds' nests.

Where to find the highest peak in the Andes mountains

When the first Spanish explorers reached the Andes mountains and began to clamber up these gigantic rocks towards Cuzco and other cities of the Incas, they were amazed by the dizzy heights of this huge range. The descriptions they wrote of what they saw are full of wonder, and yet these Spanish explorers did not even see the highest peaks of this chain of mountains, some of which rise to more than 6,000 metres.

Today we know that the tallest mountain in the Andes is Mount Aconcagua (7,035 metres). This mountain stands in the Mendoza province of north-west Argentina on the border with Chile and a little to the north of Rio de las Cuevas. From about 5,000 metres upwards this mountain is covered in eternal snows and glaciers. The glaciers are more numerous on the southern slopes where the river Aconcagua rises to flow into the Pacific Ocean. As well as being the name of a mountain and a river, Aconcagua is also the name of a province in Chile at the foot of the Andes.

Mount Aconcagua is an extinct volcano. It was climbed for the first time in 1897 by Stuart Vines and Mattias Zurbriggen who reached the summit from their base camp at Puente de Inca. Later expeditions used the same base camp because it is the best

Squirrel Monkey

place for delivering supplies.

As well as being the highest mountain in the Western Hemisphere Aconcagua is much easier to climb than other peaks in the Andes which, although lower, still resist the attempts by mountaineers from many countries to climb them.

Where sweet potatoes come from

The sweet potato is a large tuberous plant that is a native of America's central regions. Today the plant can be grown in temperate zones including parts of southern Europe.

The roots of the sweet potato are rich in sugar and have a floury texture. Root colours range from white to orange and sometimes purple inside, and from fawn to brown or red outside. The upper part of the plant consists of a stem that climbs or trails along the ground and which is from 3 to 6 metres long.

The sweet potato plant has beautiful heart-shaped leaves with long stems which are very decorative and for this reason it is sometimes grown indoors.

Where to find the world's highest lake

Of all the great lakes that lie within the various continents the highest above sea level is Lake Titicaca which is situated in a vast, high plateau on the Andes between Peru and Bolivia. The lake is 3,809 metres above sea level which is about 1,000 metres lower than the summit of Mont Blanc. It has an area of 8,135 square kilometres and is divided into two by the Strait of Tiquina. The whole lake is 178 kilometres long and is very deep (370 metres).

A number of narrow strips of land jut out into the lake from the shore and form broad stretches of sheltered water where very tall reed forests grow. The local Indians use these reeds to make boats. They also use the reeds to make big rafts which they load with soil and convert into floating gardens that produce beans, peppers, marrows, potatoes and other vegetables.

The entire region round Lake Titicaca is fairly well populated because the climate is mild and good for farming. The clear waters of the lake contain many kinds of fish.

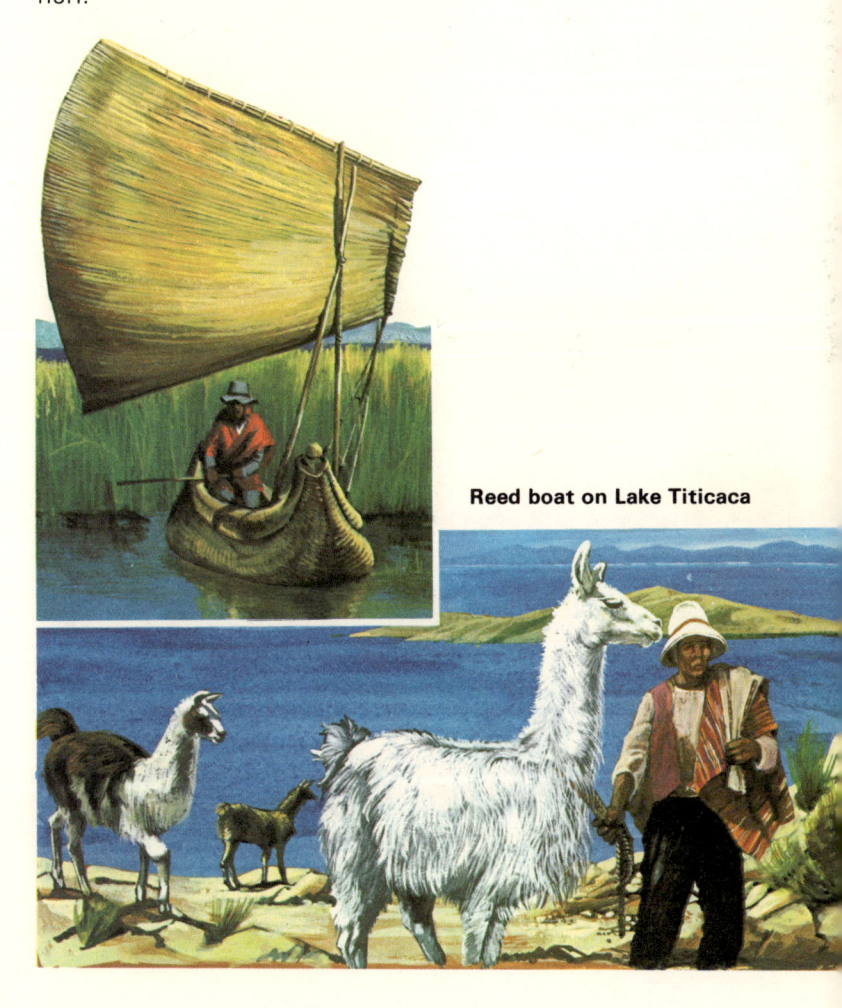

Reed boat on Lake Titicaca

115

Peruvian costumes

Where the straw is produced for Panama hats

Many people believe Panama hats are called after the country of the same name in Central America that is crossed by the famous canal. In actual fact, these hats are named after a plant that grows on the equator and which supplies the fibre that is woven into hats.

The panama plant is known to botanists under the name *Carludo-*

Panama hats originated in Peru, Bolivia and Ecuador

vica palmata which the Indians call *gigpiaga* or *apitari*. It grows in South America, especially in Bolivia, Peru and Ecuador. The plant is very ornamental and has beautiful, graceful foliage with some leaves up to 90 centimetres wide. The tough fibre for making straw hats is obtained from the young leaves of the plant.

Where the quinine tree grows wild

Quinine is a very well known drug used in the treatment of malaria. It comes from the bark of trees that grow to a height of 30 metres or more; the leaves are about 20 centimetres long and the flowers grow in red clusters. Quinine trees are natives of Peru and Bolivia. They are also cultivated in the West Indies, in Java and in the Antilles. There are many different varieties that yield quinine but they all belong to the same broad family which botanists call Cinchona.

In the early days of colonization quinine was obtained by felling the tree and stripping off its bark. The bark from the trunk of the tree and the larger branches was then cleaned and weighted down with stones to flatten it while it dried in the sun. Once the bark was dry it was packed into crates or wrapped in the fresh skin of a newly killed wild ox. When the skin dried, it shrank and stuck tight to the dried bark. This was a very bad way of gathering quinine as it created the risk of stripping entire regions of valuable trees. To avoid this danger the European colonial countries devised methods to cultivate the quinine tree in special forests.

Where to find the famous ruins of Machu Picchu

Machu Picchu, 'the lost city of the Incas', was not an important centre of the ancient Inca civilization. It was just one of the many fortified places that were built at a distance of approximately 15 kilometres from one another to defend the Inca empire against attacks by savage jungle tribes. But Machu Picchu had one big advantage: it was built completely of stone and for this reason it has survived almost intact to our own day, long after its first inhabitants abandoned it.

Machu Picchu, in a certain sense, is to the Inca civilization what the Acropolis in Athens was to the ancient Greek civilization or the Forum in Rome to the civilization of Rome. It tells us in a very vivid manner about the way of life of a civilized people who have since vanished.

Machu Picchu was discovered in 1911 by an American archaeologist, Professor Hiram Bingham, and has played an important part in understanding certain aspects of Inca history. The city stands near the river Urubamba in Peru, built on a ridge between the two peaks of Machu and Huyana Picchu, and has two very steep slopes on either side of it. The houses had sloping grass roofs and stood near palaces and temples built in different styles. There were also wells that provided water, and barracks for the soldiers. We can see in this city a smaller version of the old Inca world from which the present-day Indians who live on the Andes mountains are descended. When one sees these impressive ruins it is difficult to understand how an empire that was able to build such magnificent structures should have collapsed so suddenly.

Professor Hiram Bingham discovered Machu Picchu in 1911

Section of an aerial root of the Stanhopea orchid
- Velamen
- Cortex
- Mechanical region

Where to find the world's most beautiful orchids

There are many plants that grow in the equatorial forests of America about which little is known and there are many others which have never been seen. But there is one plant species which has such beautiful flowers that it is familiar even to people who know nothing about botany. This is the orchid group of plants estimated to contain between 15,000 and 30,000 species, many of which produce the most dazzlingly beautiful and fantastically shaped flowers.

Orchids do not grow on the ground. They are epiphytes which means that they grow on the trunks or branches of trees that have very tall trunks. The orchids are not parasites and therefore do not harm the tree they grow on, but obtain their food from the vegetable waste gathered on the tree trunk. The orchids merely use tall trees as a form of support and in order to climb upwards towards the sunlight.

The most beautiful of the wild orchids are not cultivated in greenhouses. They are looked after very carefully because their flowers are greatly prized and are the most expensive to buy.

Where the peccary lives

The peccary is a common animal of the forests of the new world, from the United States to Argentina. It resembles a small pig and is about a metre long, with thick, dark grey fur.

The variety that lives in the United States has a 'collar' of whitish-yellow hair across its chest from shoulder to shoulder. In the forests of South America, especially in Brazil, peccaries have a broad white flash that goes from the chin to the eyes.

The male peccary's canine teeth protrude from its mouth and turn downwards. The peccary is a gregarious animal and likes to live in groups of between ten and 100. Often, large herds wander through the forests in search of food. Like the wild boar of Europe, peccaries eat almost everything, including poisonous snakes as they are immune to the venom.

Where the opossum lives

The opossum is the only marsupial animal living on the American continent. Marsupials are mammals which have a special pouch on their stomachs where they keep their babies. Inside the pouch are the mammary glands where the baby marsupials suck their mother's milk. The best-known marsupial is the kangaroo, but there are many other kinds, most of them living in Oceania in the region of the Pacific Ocean.

The opossum lives in Central America. It is about the same size as a cat and has coarse fur in grey and yellowish bands and a white face with large, dark eyes and black, mottled ears. The opossum has a long tail with which it hangs from branches of trees while leaving its paws free to catch its prey. The mother opossum usually carries the young on her back as soon as they have moved out of the pouch. She puts her tail up over her back so that the babies can hold on to it with their own little tails as the animals move along.

The opossum lives for about eight years. When in danger it often pretends to be dead ('plays possum') until the trouble has passed.

Where to find the country with the fewest roads

The country among developed nations with the fewest roads in relation to its total surface is Brazil. This nation is still largely covered by dense virgin forests through which it is extremely difficult to build roads. The Brazilian government is at present constructing a major roadway system that will cross territories not previously reached by modern civilization, cutting the forest into two as it runs straight through it. But even after such a gigantic task Brazil will still remain a country of few roads and the aeroplane will continue to be the best means of transport and communication over vast distances, as it is today. Brasilia, the new capital of Brazil that was opened in 1960 on a high plateau in the interior, runs the risk of dying as a city because of the lack of roads to link it with other cities. This would be a great pity because Brasilia was designed to be the most modern city in the world, with its buildings constructed to the most advanced designs and techniques of city planning.

The young opossum hold on to their mother's tail as they all move along

The Belem-Brasilia highway

Blue and Yellow Macaw

Hyacinthine Macaw

Red and Yellow Macaw

Where the brightly coloured macaw lives

The world's largest parrots live in the forests round the Amazon River. They are the macaws, birds with splendidly coloured plumage that can be seen in any zoo, making a terrible din with their harsh, squawking cries.

The macaw, which lives in a region that stretches from Mexico to Bolivia, can grow to more than a metre in length from its beak to the tip of its tail. Two varieties noted for their size are the blue and yellow macaw (*Ara ararauna*) and the green macaw (*Ara militaris*). Macaws have an amazing display of colours, all of them very bright and contrasting with one another.

Parrots are common in the forests and open spaces of tropical zones in the southern hemisphere, except in southern Africa. There are more than 300 species, including bantam and giant varieties. Parrots all have the same kind of large, strong, curved beak which they use to crack open the hard shell of fruits that they live on. All parrots also have identical claws with the first and fourth toes turned backwards, enabling them to keep a tight hold when they perch on trees. They are tree-dwelling birds but they are also very good fliers.

Where the first potatoes were discovered

The potato is a native of Chile and Peru where the local inhabitants had grown it for a long time before the first Europeans arrived. The Spaniards first came across the potato plant during their conquest of America and they brought it to Europe. It was many years before this new vegetable became commonly known. It was only towards the end of the eighteenth century that potatoes began to be cultivated on a large scale in Europe.

The potato plant has a herbaceous stalk about 60 centimetres long and oval leaves that are whitish underneath. The part of the plant that is eaten is not the fruit, but merely the underground part of the stalk. This is known as the tuber and acts as a storage place for the substances needed to feed the plant.

The ancient Incas knew of some sixty different varieties of potato, all of them adapted to growing in differing weather conditions. In this way the Incas could grow potatoes near desert land or at altitudes of more than 4,000 metres near Lake Titicaca.

The potato is eaten as a vegetable and is also used to produce a type of flour, dextrin and alcohol.

Where the Brazil nut grows

The Brazil nut is a large woody nut which, with its three sides, rather resembles the slice of a mandarin orange. Inside the dark, rough shell lies a hard, white kernel which has a sweetish taste.

The tree on which the Brazil nut grows is the *Bertholletia*

excelsa, also called the Pará nut tree, which grows in the forests around the Amazon River in Brazil. The tree must have a hot, humid climate and it cannot be grown in Europe even under hot-house conditions. It has evergreen leaves and is tall and majestic, growing to a height of more than 40 metres.

The Brazil nut is not really a fruit but a seed. From fifteen to twenty of these seeds are contained inside the real fruit which acts as a capsule or covering. This capsule is large, round and woody with a soft husk.

The Brazil nut is a very important food for the Indians who live in Brazil. It also provides a valuable oil which can be used as a foodstuff or for lubricating delicate machinery. Because of their high oil content Brazil nuts tend to turn sour quickly.

Where the jaguar lurks

The jaguar is one of the best-known members of the cat family in America, living at the edge of the forests in marshy regions of tropical zones. The ground colour of its coat varies from white to black but most jaguars are orange-brown in colour, the black spots arranged in rosettes with a black spot in the centre.

The jaguar resembles the leopard but is more heavily built. It hunts its prey by night and can catch its food by fishing in rivers or pouncing on monkeys or birds in trees, for this animal is a skilful climber and a good swimmer. Cattle or horses are its favourite victims and for this reason the jaguar is a threat to remote farms where livestock grazes in the open.

The jaguar will also attack

Jaguars can swim with ease and often do so whenever it is necessary to catch their prey

people and tear them apart as a tiger does. It is a very fierce animal and difficult to tame, even if captured while still very young. In its attacks on other animals the jaguar displays a strength and ferocity much greater than that of the big cats of Africa and Asia.

Where to find the splendid bay of the River Plate

The broad and beautiful bay of the River Plate opens out on to the Atlantic Ocean. The bay is where the river Paraná empties into the ocean and also forms the border between Uruguay and Argentina. Another great river, the Uruguay, also flows into the bay. The combined waters of these two rivers form a large area of fresh water amid the salty ocean.

The River Plate gets its name from the Spanish word *plata*, meaning 'silver'. Early explorers called it 'the river of silver' after they met members of wild Indian tribes wearing wonderful silver jewellery. Later the explorers discovered the jewellery was the property of a Portuguese expedition slaughtered by the Indians.

It was in the bay of the River Plate that the German pocket battleship *Graf Spee* was scuttled during the Second World War.

The Orinoco is one of the largest rivers in South America

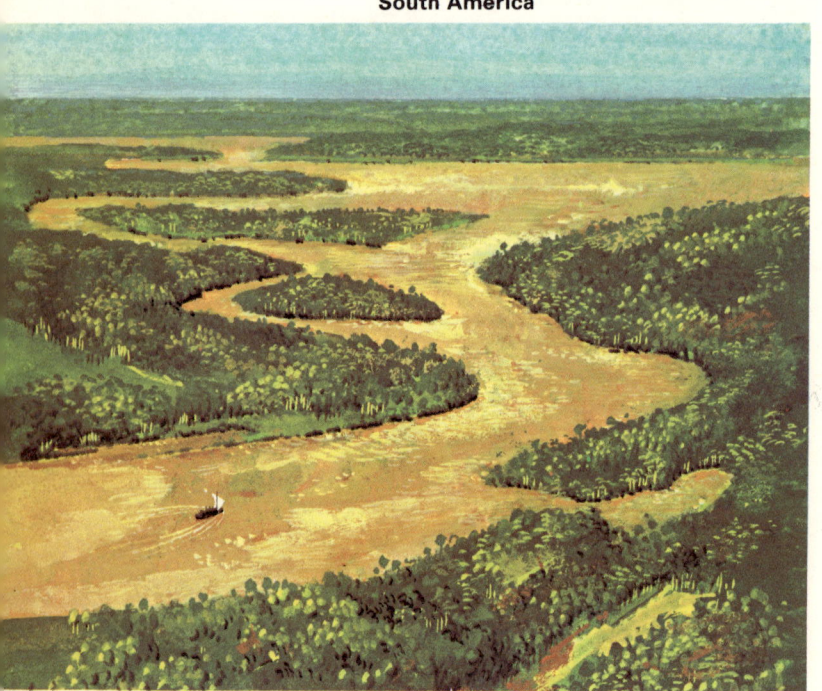

Where the pawpaw grows

The pawpaw is an evergreen plant with large leaves and brown to dark red flowers, which resembles a tree and grows to a height of more than 12 metres. The plant, also known as a melon tree because of its fruit, grows in a natural state in tropical regions of America. Today it is grown wherever the climate allows because of the commercial value of its fruit.

Pawpaw fruit resembles a cocoa bean in shape and in the way that it is attached very close to the trunk of the tree. But the pawpaw fruit is more like a melon, with yellow flesh, rich in vitamins, and lots of juice. A large pawpaw can weigh up to 10 kilogrammes. The flesh of the fruit can be eaten raw or used to make jams, sweets or beverages.

Where manioc is eaten

Manioc is little-known in Europe although this plant could easily grow there. It is very common in tropical zones, especially where potatoes and cereals such as wheat find it difficult to grow.

The manioc plant is a shrub that grows from about 1 to 3 metres in length with large, spreading, long-stalked leaves. It blooms in summer and produces fruit containing large, greyish seeds, rich in oil. This is extracted by crushing the fruit and is used in making certain medicines.

The most valuable part of the manioc plant are the large, tapering roots which grow up to a metre in length and from 15 to 20 centimetres in diameter. They contain a flour-like substance and weigh as much as 10 kilogrammes.

Manioc tubers are poisonous if eaten raw because they contain hydrocyanic acid, but are quite harmless when cooked and make a wholesome food. The roots produce a kind of flour called tapioca which is very nourishing. South American Indians have eaten tapioca for thousands of years.

Innumerable people living in tropical lands throughout the world eat manioc. The plant is a native of Brazil, but it is now grown also in Africa and Asia. Manioc is also known as cassava.

Where head-hunters live

The Jivaros are the most feared of the wild Indians of South America. They live on the lower east slopes of the Andes in eastern Ecuador and Peru. Many of them have fair complexions and reddish hair and are the descendants of Europeans who interbred with Indians many years ago. They drive away evil spirits by painting their faces red and wearing special, protective charms and amulets.

These Indians are so suspicious that they even have their huts many kilometres apart from one another. Only when they are threatened by a major attack do they come together and elect a chief. A Jivaro father's main duty is to keep alive in his sons a sense of revenge against the family's enemies.

Head-hunting, for which these people are notorious, is part of their religious beliefs. The Jivaros think that every warrior inherits the soul of a dead ancestor who is supposed to appear in a dream to the young warrior during his period of initiation. The warrior keeps this soul for a certain number of years before inheriting another one, but if he should lose his soul he will forfeit all his protection against disease and people who wish him harm. The only way to defend himself is to take the soul of an enemy and cut off his head. The Jivaro then shrinks the human head to about the size of an orange and hangs it as a trophy outside his hut.

Head-shrinkers at work and (right) a shrunken head with the lips sewn up and eyes removed

Three examples of Argentinian costume

Where maté is the national drink

Everybody in Europe knows about tea and coffee: in South America everybody knows about maté, the national drink of Paraguay, Brazil and other countries.

Maté, also known as Paraguay tea, is obtained by drying the branches and leaves of a small tree that resembles holly. This tree grows in a natural state from about 500 to 1,000 metres above sea level on the hills around the rivers Paraná, Paraguay and Uruguay. The tree is about 6 metres high. In some regions which have a hot and very humid climate, the maté tree forms most of the undergrowth of the big forests. The maté tree is widely cultivated in certain regions of South America because it is important in local trade. Although it had been used since early times by the Indians, the Jesuits were the first to cultivate it, which is why it is sometimes called Jesuits' tea. Once the leaves have been gathered and dried, they are roasted and reduced to a powder which is then matured to produce a pleasant aroma.

It takes only a small amount of this powder to prepare the maté beverage. This is made by pouring boiling, sweetened water over the maté inside special containers which are usually pumpkin-like gourds which have been hollowed out. Maté is drunk from the container through a tube like a drinking-straw.

The ancient Incas drank maté this way long before the first Europeans discovered America. Maté, like tea and coffee, contains the drug caffeine which acts as a stimulant on the nervous system. It is a beverage that has not proved popular in Europe.

Where to find avocado plants

Avocado trees are evergreens that vary in shape and size. In their natural state they grow in tropical and sub-tropical zones of America. The trunk of the tree is from 10 to 20 metres tall and the foliage is always thick and a beautiful dark green in colour. A strange feature of this plant is that it blooms constantly from autumn to spring.

The avocado gets its name from the mispronunciation of its original Aztec name *ahuacatl*. The fruit which became known to Europeans in the sixteenth century, has long been eaten by the natives of Central America because it is a good substitute for meat. The flesh of this fruit is not only very rich in vitamins but has a very high fat content that provides more calories than bananas and other nourishing fruits.

Where the rubber tree grows wild

The most useful plants that grow wild in the tropical forests of America are those of the *Hevea* family which are also known as rubber trees. The first explorer to describe these plants was Charles de la Condamine who lectured to the French Academy about them in 1736.

The Indians of South America called the rubber tree *cau-uchu* which means 'weeping wood'. This was because the rubber tree produces latex, a sticky, milky fluid which becomes solid, hard and elastic when it dries. Rubber as we know it is the result of certain processes which the latex undergoes. The fluid is extracted by cutting the bark of the tree and letting the latex run into cups.

Where the condor lives

Condors are big vultures that live in the mountainous areas of North and South America. Like almost all vultures, condors have no feathers on their heads and necks but where the neck is joined to the rest of the bird's body there is a broad collar of thick soft plumage. The feathers on the wings and tail are very strong and these birds are marvellous fliers.

There are two main types of condor: the Californian and the Andean. The Californian condor lives in the Rocky Mountains where it has been almost completely wiped out by hunters so that it is now one of the world's rarest birds. The Andean condor inhabits the huge mountain chain of the Andes in South America and has been hunted less so that more of these birds exist. The condor is incredibly tough and can glide for hours and stand up to the great changes in air pressure that occur at altitudes of about 5,000 metres where this bird flies.

Where to find the cold waters of the Humboldt current

Everybody knows about the Gulf Stream, the great warm current that flows across the Atlantic Ocean to the shores of northern Europe and helps to keep the winter climate of those European regions mild. There are other ocean currents which are not so well known but also have an important influence on the climate of vast territories. One of these is the Humboldt which flows from the cold regions of the Antarctic to the western coast of South America. The Humboldt current then mingles with the warmer waters of the equator.

The chief effect of the Humboldt current is to make the South American coastal area between the Andes and the Pacific Ocean into a region of dry deserts. This is because rain-bearing clouds unload their moisture when they condense against the cold air from the Humboldt current. When these clouds reach the coast they have no moisture left and so the coastal areas receive rain only in exceptional circumstances.

The Humboldt current is called after the scientist who was the first to make a complete study of it, Alexander von Humboldt (1769–1859), a great explorer and naturalist. He first discovered the great importance that this cold current had for the climate of the region. Humboldt was also the creator of phytogeography which is the study of plant life in relation to climatic, physical, biological and geological factors.

Alexander von Humboldt, explorer and naturalist

Where they build houses for snakes

The snakes are kept under special domes resembling igloos

Strange as it may seem, there are places where poisonous snakes, one of man's deadliest enemies, are reared and looked after with great care by people. These snakes even have special houses, resembling igloos, built for them.

This 'snake city' has a purpose: it enables scientists to study the habits of reptiles and the effect of their venom. In this way the scientists can prepare the antidote, the substance which will save a poisoned person from dying of a snake bite.

The most famous snake centre is the modern Butantan Institute of São Paulo in Brazil. This was founded to study snake serum in an attempt to reduce the high number of deaths from poisonous snake bites. Some of Brazil's poisonous snakes are among the world's most deadly and aggressive and these are bred at the Institute. By studying their venom a large number of antidotes have been produced, including one with a very wide application which is used when the person bitten cannot remember what kind of snake was responsible.

Where the giant *Megatherium* lived millions of years ago

The fossilized remains of these gigantic animals, the ancestors of today's sloths, are commonly found throughout Central and South America where they lived until about a million years ago.

The *Megatherium* was an enormous mammal, more than 5 metres high, which looked rather like a bear. Its squat body was covered in rough fur and when the animal stood up straight on its hind legs it supported itself against its short and very muscular tail. The *Megatherium* had a long head, deep-set eyes and a huge mouth that gave it a terrifying appearance, but examination of its teeth shows that the *Megatherium* was not ferocious and did not eat the flesh of other animals. It lived on leaves which it obtained by pulling down the branches of trees with its powerful front paws. It also ate certain roots which it dug up with its claws.

The *Megatherium* did not move very fast but relied on its huge size and strong claws to defend itself.

Megatherium

The great lake of Maracaibo

Gaucho on the Argentinian pampas

Where to find the great petrol lake

In 1499 the Italian explorer Amerigo Vespucci explored the coast of South America. When he came to the great lake of Maracaibo, he believed he had come to a lagoon similar to that of Venice in Italy, so he called the region Little Venice. In Spanish this is Venezuela, and that is the name of the country today. Vespucci probably had no idea that one day Venezuela's greatest wealth would come from that lake.

Maracaibo covers an area of 13,000 square kilometres and is the biggest lake in South America. In the early 1900s huge deposits of petroleum were discovered at the bottom of the lake and since 1917 the petroleum has been extracted by thousands of oil wells drilled under the water. Because of these petroleum deposits Venezuela is the biggest petroleum producer in the world after the United States and the Soviet Union. It is also the world's greatest exporter of oil.

Where to find the immense 'green sea' of the Americas

The 'green sea' is the name that has been given to the Argentinian pampas, an endless plain of very rich green grass stretching from the foothills of the Andes mountains in the west to the coast of the Atlantic Ocean in the east. The rivers that flow through the plain are slow, often forming large areas of stagnant water which become swamps covered in reed forests.

The plain is dusty in places and during the fierce summer storms the winds whip up huge clouds of very fine dust. The pampas are farmed only in certain places which are sheltered and receive enough rain. They are an ideal place for grazing cattle and are the domain of the *gauchos*, the skilful cowboys of South America who look after herds of thousands of animals. Today cattle-breeding in the pampas is going through a difficult period but meat is still one of Argentina's biggest sources of wealth.

Armadillo and (right) rolled into a ball

Where armadillos live

The armadillo is a strange mammal that is common throughout South America. It is covered in a kind of armour composed of solid plates and movable bands which go round its body so that the animal can roll up into a ball. The number of these bands varies from species to species: the best-known armadillo, the peba, which can also be found in North America, has nine bands. The head of the armadillo is protected by a horny helmet and its tail resembles a knight's sword and is kept inside a sheath which is jointed so that the animal can move the tail.

There is one variety of armadillo that lives in the pampas of South America whose tail is so short that it can scarcely be seen. This is the *Chlamyphorus truncatus*, also known as the *pichiciego*, a small armadillo about 15 centimetres long with pink scales which cover only part of its body.

Giant Armadillo

Where the shells of the glyptodons were found

Armadillos are usually little creatures which live in almost every part of South America. They are the direct descendants of the glyptodon, a giant animal that lived many millions of years ago.

The glyptodon was a peaceful animal. It was able to protect itself against the terrible monsters of those days because of its stout shell which covered its entire body. It defended itself rather as the armadillos do today, or even the tortoises. Whilst it was under attack the glyptodon would withdraw into its shell and stay there until its enemy grew tired of waiting. If the enemy refused to go away, the glyptodon would then use its strong tail like a club. This tail was covered in sharp spikes that could do much damage.

Many fossilized shells of glyptodons have been found in the plains of South America. These animals first appeared about 40 million years ago but we do not know exactly when they became extinct to make way for more advanced forms of animal life. They still wandered the Earth when the first human beings appeared.

It is quite possible that the shells of glyptodons were used as homes by primitive peoples. These shells were more than 4 metres long and a human skeleton was once found lying underneath one. Beneath other glyptodon shells have been found ashes and the remains of fires that men must have lit, with flints and other man-made objects beside them.

Where the *burití* race takes place

In the heart of Brazil, where the forests end and the grassy plains begin, live the Kraho Indians who were robbed of their hunting grounds by the white people. From the air a Kraho village looks like a big wheel: the white sandy road round the houses is the rim of the wheel and the village roads form the spokes, each road running from a house to the square at the centre of the village. The Kraho Indians have an old legend which says that they are the descendants of the Sun and Moon who were hunters and quarrelled about taking a wife. For this reason the Kraho tribe today is divided into two parties.

During the hunting season the Kraho leave their village and camp out in the plains. They share whatever they catch and they also keep something for members of the tribe who cannot hunt. But whoever in the tribe fails to come back with a dead animal from the hunt becomes the laughing stock. When the hunt is over the Kraho give thanks to their gods in a picturesque sporting competition: the *burití* race. The *burití* is the trunk of a palm tree weighing about 90 kilogrammes. The competitors form two teams and race against each other to carry the trunk to the village. The winner is the man who is first to throw the palm trunk in front of the patron lady of the festival.

Where to find the longest road in the world

America is a continent of records, huge construction schemes and the continent which has the longest road in the world. This is part of the Pan American Highway System and links the distant northern regions of the American continent with Tierra del Fuego in the southernmost tip of South America with an extremely long ribbon of road.

Work on the Pan American Highway System began in 1923. The longest road runs for almost 22,300 kilometres, from Anchorage in Alaska to southern Chile, following the Pacific coast for most of its extent.

Glyptodon

Highway in Caracas

THE WHERE OF OCEANIA

Where to find pigeons that 'suckle' their young

The blue-crowned pigeon, or Queen Victoria crowned pigeon as it is also called, is a close relative of our pigeons and is the largest member of this family of birds. It is about the size of a small turkey, with long, very strong legs and beautifully coloured feathers. On its head is a lace-like crest that is always upright and looks just like a crown.

The blue-crowned pigeon lives in the forests and swamps of New Guinea, feeding on worms, grubs and seeds which it pecks up from the ground. Whenever danger arises it flies up to the highest branches in the trees and utters sad, gloomy cries.

Like all pigeons this bird 'suckles' its young. Just before the young pigeons are hatched from their eggs their mother begins to produce a thick fluid known as 'milk'. This fluid is produced from two pouches inside the bird's throat and is the only form of food that the baby birds receive during the first three weeks of their life. The young birds instinctively poke their beaks into their mother's wide-open beak and gather up the nourishing milk fluid produced from the pouches.

Where to find the main religious centre of Polynesia

At one time Raiatea, the largest of the Iles Sous le Vent in the Society Islands, was the religious and political centre of all Polynesia. The big canoes with their outriggers carrying huge sails made of pandanus leaves travelled for thousands of kilometres across the open Pacific to reach the lagoon of Raiatea.

Many religious relics have been found in Raiatea: one of them, which lies abandoned in thick forest, is the *mare*, a grim altar made of black stone. It lies along a line running east to west that follows the path of the Sun god

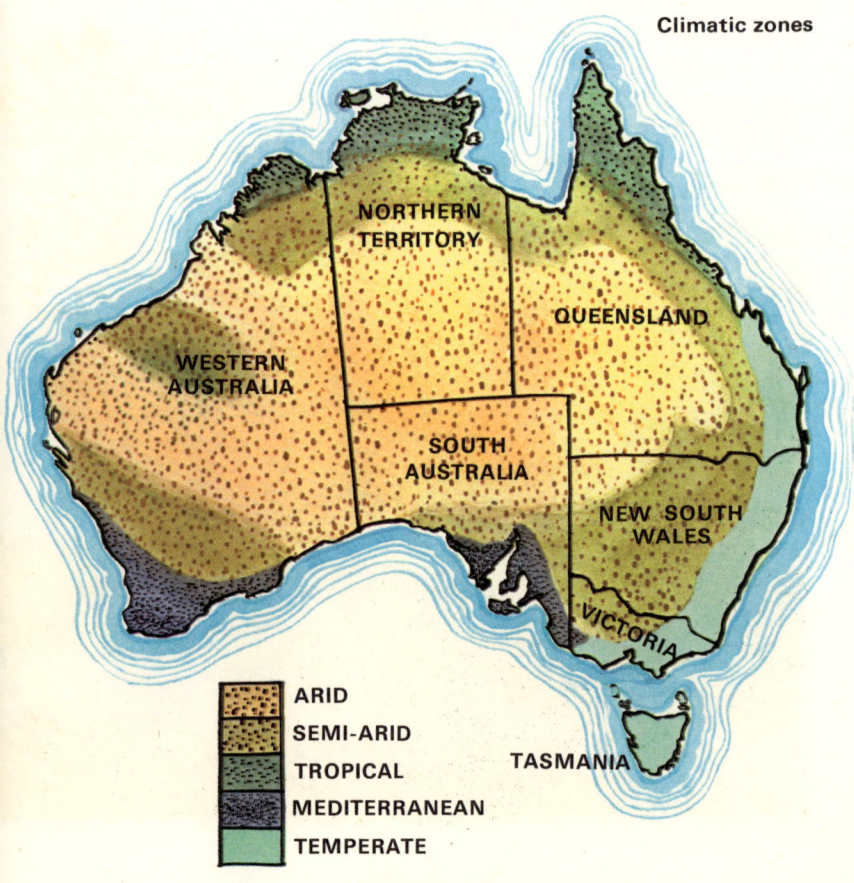

Climatic zones

- ARID
- SEMI-ARID
- TROPICAL
- MEDITERRANEAN
- TEMPERATE

in the heavens. It was on this altar that the priests sacrificed their victims. Raiatea still has the Stone of the Chiefs, a stone pillar more than 2 metres high. The Polynesian chiefs used to stand against the pillar when they held their meetings on the island and whoever was taller than the pillar was elected King of Kings and High Priest.

The existence of these extremely tall men has been proved by the large bones found in the burial places of ancient warriors. Raiatea is also famous for its *tiki*, colossal images made of wood or stone which watched over the people and ensured the fertility of the soil. The most sacred *tiki* were in the centre of the island and kept under the waters of the lagoon. The ancient Polynesians regarded this as the most sacred point of the universe where the land and the oceans began.

Where budgerigars come from

Budgerigars are brightly coloured miniature parrots which are a very popular cagebird and are kept as pets in many homes. These birds are specially bred but their natural home is Australia where many can be seen flying free in forests. In the wild this little parrot has pale green feathers on its back and bright green plumage on its chest, but selective breeding has developed yellow, grey, violet, blue and green varieties. Like all members of the parrot family it has a long tapering tail and a slender and graceful body.

In Australia budgerigars live together in large groups in forests and plains, fluttering from tree to tree. They are very tame and can be easily domesticated and

Budgerigars, native birds of Australia

live quite happily in a cage. These birds do not require any special care and are easy to breed. Once they become a family pet, budgerigars rarely want to leave their home. They are often allowed to come out of their cages but care must be taken that there are no cats around to attack them.

Budgerigars in flight

Where to find black swans

The beautiful black swan is so common round the coasts of Australia that it has become the emblem on the government coat-of-arms of Western Australia. In this region there are many black swans which live in lakes along the coast. They have also been introduced into New Zealand.

Like the white swans of the northern hemisphere, black swans are splendid swimmers. They prefer to stay in one place close to where they were born and are the only swans which do not migrate.

During the nesting season black swans build a large nest among the reeds on an island lake. The nest is simply a heap of twigs with a hollow in it. The eggs are laid and hatched between August and December which are the spring months in the southern hemisphere. The baby swans are covered in grey, downy feathers and are very lively, learning to swim within a few hours. They eat grubs, insects and molluscs scooped up by their mother's beak and ride on her back, nestling down in the soft feathers between her wings.

Spiny Anteater, showing the egg pouch

Where to find mammals that lay eggs

Oceania is a place full of surprises in the animal kingdom. In this region there still live the last examples of prehistoric creatures, odd-looking animals with strange habits who, because of the isolation of this part of the world, have retained the features of their weird ancestors of millions of years ago.

One of the strangest and most mysterious of these animals is the spiny anteater which lives in the sandy and rocky regions of south-eastern Australia and in Tasmania. The spiny anteater is an odd mixture: it has sharp quills like a porcupine, an elongated beak-like snout and feet shaped like those of an elephant. The feet have powerful claws and the animal has a long, thin, sticky tongue like other anteaters. When the spiny anteater is in danger it rolls up into a ball or rapidly digs itself a hole where it hides so that it is difficult to take the animal by surprise and watch it.

The spiny anteater lives on insects. Its favourite food is ants and termites which it scoops up with its long, sticky tongue. The animal uses its strong claws to tear ant-hills apart or to break down the hard clay dwellings of termites.

Like the duck-billed platypus,

this strange mammal lays eggs. But the spiny anteater carries its eggs in a special pouch in its skin until they are hatched. The babies stay inside their mother's pouch where they suck her milk through special hairs on her body. As soon as the babies grow quills of their own which prick the mother, she makes them leave the pouch and become independent.

Where to find the great deserts of Australia

The eastern coast of Australia is a fertile region with plenty of rain and a mild climate. These good conditions are caused by the Great Dividing Range, or Eastern Highlands as it is also called, a chain of mountains that runs all the way from north to south forming a narrow coastal plain. These mountains act as a barrier to the trade winds from the Pacific Ocean, so that when the clouds reach them they let fall their rain on the coastal region.

But just as the Great Dividing Range makes the coastal plain fertile it also makes the land to the west into a desolate, arid desert. Once the clouds have crossed the mountains they have no more rain left for Australia's central regions so that this land is all desert with only a few thorny acacia trees dotted around.

About two-thirds of the total land area of Australia is desert in which human life is impossible. The biggest deserts are the Great Sandy Desert in the north-west, and the Great Victoria Desert in the south, both of which are almost completely flat and present an ugly and monotonous landscape.

The supply and conservation of water are among Australia's greatest problems. The aridity of the interior is relieved by the presence of artesian wells, including the Great Australian or Artesian basin which is the largest artesian area in the world.

About two-thirds of the land in Australia is desert

Tree Kangaroo

Where to find kangaroos that climb trees

Of the many kinds of kangaroo that live in Australia one of the strangest is the kangaroo that climbs trees to eat the fruit and tender shoots. Unlike ordinary kangaroos, this animal has much bigger front legs which are almost as well developed as its hind ones. The tree kangaroo also has sharp claws to help it clamber among the trees with all the acrobatic skill of a monkey.

Like all marsupials, kangaroos give birth to tiny, helpless babies which must be placed immediately into the warmth of the mother's pouch, but they have to find it by themselves. To help the baby, the mother kangaroo uses her tongue to leave a long wet trail of saliva along her stomach which leads to her pouch. The baby kangaroo, pink and hairless, begins to climb up his mother's stomach by holding on to the fur, instinctively following the wet trail until it reaches the opening of its mother's pouch and creeps inside.

Where rabbits are a public menace

Until the 1850s there were no rabbits at all in Australia. Then it was decided to import some of these animals and breed them as food. After several attempts at introduction three pairs of breeding rabbits were let loose in New South Wales. This turned out to be the greatest disaster for Australian farmers for the rabbits settled down so happily in their new surroundings and produced so many litters of young rabbits, that soon the entire continent was invaded by them. Farmers' crops faced the danger of being completely eaten up and it was estimated that between 1876 and 1885 rabbits caused millions of pounds worth of damage.

Rabbits breed extremely rapidly. A female can produce up to twelve baby rabbits every forty days. In this way, under perfect conditions, a pair of rabbits can in three years produce 13 million rabbits. In order to fight this terrible threat tall wire fences were built to keep the rabbits away from cultivated fields, but the rabbits burrowed underneath them. Today rabbits are hunted mercilessly in Australia and every year many millions are killed.

Where to find Australia's richest mines

Almost every month in recent years news comes of the discovery of new major mineral deposits in Australia which will be exploited in the future. The Australian government has launched a broad research programme to survey the land and draw up a complete list of its natural resources. The plan is revealing that this immense territory is one of the richest in the world for the many kinds of natural wealth that lie underneath its soil.

It was already discovered during the second half of the nineteenth century that some zones, especially Queensland and Western Australia, were rich in valuable minerals. Australia, too, had its 'gold fever' which attracted many people in search of this precious metal. Gold was certainly abundant in Australia but it was not the only form of natural wealth. Australia is also rich in such minerals as tungsten, manganese, cobalt, and uranium. It is the world's greatest producer of lead and possesses vast quantities of zinc, gold, silver, tungsten and lignite. Iron ore is widely distributed throughout the country.

Australia's most important mineral deposits today are at Mount Isa in Queensland and at Broken Hill in New South Wales. New deposits are being found in other zones, however, especially on the eastern coastal strip where large deposits of coal also occur.

Australia is rich in minerals because many of this country's rocks are among the oldest in the world. The minerals have been produced in these rocks through the geological processes that have taken place over thousands of millions of years.

Kalgoorlie Gold Mine

Where the screw pine grows

One plant grown in hothouses in Europe is the *Pandanus*, commonly known as the screw pine, many varieties of which are found in the islands of Polynesia. The stem sprouts roots some distance above the ground; these grow downwards to the soil, forming props which help to support the plant.

Pandanus leaves have no stalks and grow in spirals round the twisted branches of the plant. The people of Oceania eat the shoot that grows at the heart of these leaves as a vegetable because it has an aromatic flavour. The tender leaves of the *Pandanus* are rather like cabbage and can be eaten raw or cooked. Some parts of the older and tougher leaves can also be eaten.

The most important quality of *Pandanus* leaves is that they can be woven into mats, baskets, sails and fans.

Sydney Cove

Where to find Australia's main cities

The climate of Australia has determined to a large extent where the people live. The entire central region and much of the western zones are deserts and very inhospitable. The eastern coast has a good climate and this is why most Australians live there.

More than 7 million Australians, or more than half of the country's total population, live in large cities. Sydney and Melbourne have the most inhabitants and their combined population is almost 5 million. We can say, then, that more than one-third of the population of Australia is concentrated within its two main cities.

Sydney, which is Australia's chief port, is situated astride a long inlet. It is a fine city of skyscrapers, bold modern buildings and many parks. It was founded in 1788 and the two halves of the city are joined by the famous Sidney Harbour Bridge, one of the largest steel-arch bridges in the world. The bridge is some 135 metres above the water and has a span of about 503 metres. The city of Melbourne, named after the British prime minister, Lord Melbourne, is also on the coast and is the outlet for a rich farming region. Canberra is an entirely new city and is the capital of Australia. The building of the city began in 1913 to the plans of the American architect, Walter Burley Griffin, and the city was formally declared open in 1927. Canberra, which has a large number of parks and gardens, is situated at the foot of the Australian Alps in an area of many artificial lakes.

The frilled lizard with its frill displayed and (right) running on its hind legs

Where to find frilled lizards

To have an idea of what the frilled lizard looks like you must imagine a lizard with its head poking through an open and brightly coloured umbrella.

This strange monster lives in Australia and is really only a big lizard with a large fold of skin round its neck. Normally this red frill hangs like a cape about the lizard's shoulders so that it is scarcely noticeable, but when the creature is excited or frightened it billows out the frill which has bones inside it rather like the ribs of an umbrella. At the same time the lizard usually opens its jaws wide to reveal a saffron-yellow interior and very sharp teeth. The creature also hisses like an angry cat and the whole effect can be quite frightening. But this is all bluff to scare off enemies, for the frilled lizard does not really frighten anyone. If its enemy does not show any signs of running away, this ugly reptile takes to its heels in fright. As it runs away the frilled lizard shows that it is a relation of those terrible flesh-eating dinosaurs that lived millions of years ago: it runs on its hind legs only, flicking its tail from side to side as it moves to keep its balance. This is the way that the dinosaurs moved.

The frilled lizard lives in the trees and feeds on insects.

Where to find the only bird with a strong sense of smell

The kiwi is a very primitive bird, descended from the big, wingless birds that lived on the Earth millions of years ago. The last surviving members of this family of birds now live only in the forests of New Zealand where they are carefully protected to prevent their becoming extinct.

The kiwi has a long, slender beak which it uses for poking about in the ground to find the worms, insects and grubs that it feeds on. During the day the kiwi stays hidden in dense shrubbery or in holes it digs in the ground, coming out at night to hunt for its food. It is the only bird with a strong sense of smell and can sniff out its food at great distances.

The kiwi, which is greyish-brown in colour and about the size of a chicken, is the national emblem of New Zealand.

Academy of Science, Canberra

137

Where Captain Cook travelled on his voyages of exploration

James Cook, born in England in 1728, served as an officer in the Royal Navy and became the most famous explorer of his day and one of the greatest of all time. He had a thorough knowledge of the maps and charts that then existed and was appointed to lead an expedition to make a scientific study of the passage of the planet Venus across the Sun as observed from the South Seas.

Cook left England on 25 August 1768, on board his ship the *Endeavour*. He sailed to Madeira and then on to Rio de Janeiro. From there he rounded Cape Horn and in April 1769 he reached Tahiti. He sailed all round New Zealand and passed through the strait which was named after him. He returned home via the previously unknown eastern coast of Australia.

In a second voyage that began in 1772, Cook discovered southern Polynesia and explored stretches of the Australian coast. He also discovered many groups of islands including New Caledonia.

Cook returned to England in 1775 where he received many honours. Soon the longing to go back to sea came upon him again and he set sail on what turned out to be his last adventure. In 1776 he reached New Zealand. From there he set out for Hawaii to look for new sea routes and new lands but he was killed by islanders in Hawaii on 14 February 1779.

Where to find the flying phalanger

The flying phalanger, or sugar glider, is a small squirrel-like animal that lives in Australia. It is about 50 centimetres long, varying in colour from dark brown to bluish-grey, and has a very sweet tooth. Its chief foods are fruits with a high sugar content and the sweet nectar of flowers.

The flying phalanger lives in eucalyptus or gum trees. It is a very shy animal and runs away if anyone approaches it.

The animal builds its nest among the leafy branches of the trees. The nest is made of twigs and branches roughly woven together in the shape of a ball. These nests provide shelter for the baby flying phalangers after they come out of their mothers' pouches.

The baby phalangers are very funny. They never stand still for a minute but jump and tumble about so much that they pull their nest apart. The mother makes them repair the damage before they go out in search of food at night. If some of the nest material has been lost, the children have to go and gather more twigs and leaves from the surrounding branches.

Captain Cook

Where sheep graze by the million

The region immediately to the west of Australia's Great Dividing Range receives whatever is left of the rainfall brought by the trade winds from the Pacific Ocean. Much of the rain falls first on the coastal plain east of the mountain range so that the land on the other side of the range receives much less rain. This makes farming difficult but there is enough rain to produce immense areas of grasslands which are ideal for feeding large herds of animals. The zone that runs from the Gulf of Carpentaria in the north of Australia to Adelaide in the south, is one gigantic grazing ground where millions of head of livestock, especially sheep, roam freely.

Sheep represent one of Australia's main sources of wealth. There are some 160 million of them, most of them Merino which produce excellent wool. Merino sheep were first imported into Australia from Spain in 1797 and now form about 70 per cent of Australia's total sheep population. Australia is the world's main supplier of wool. The size of the country and the variation in climate allow sheep shearing to be carried on throughout the year.

Where to find the Australian anteater

The Australian anteater is one of the country's marsupials and an extremely strange animal. It is about 30 centimetres long with a slender body, short legs and a feathery tail. Its greyish-brown coat is banded with several light-coloured stripes on its back.

The Australian anteater's ancestors first appeared during the Jurassic Period, about 180 million years ago when the huge dinosaurs roamed the Earth. Zoologists study this animal carefully for it really belongs to a world that died many millions of years ago.

This marsupial has no pouch but a slight fold of skin on its belly. It feeds almost entirely on ants, catching them by darting out its long, sticky, worm-like tongue. Although it has teeth the Australian anteater does not chew its food but squashes it against the roof of its mouth before swallowing it. The animal moves along the ground in little hops rather like a squirrel.

Australian Anteater

Sandy or Agile Wallaby

Black-gloved Wallaby

Where the kangaroo is hunted

The grassy plains of central Australia are the home of the kangaroo which roams in herds, moving along slowly in search of pasture. Some of the old kangaroos act as look-outs from special vantage points, and whenever they spot the slightest sign of danger approaching they sound the alarm by thumping their powerful tails on the ground.

After the kangaroos have eaten their fill, they lie down and sleep on the grass in the warmth of the sun. This is when the hunters take them by surprise.

Aborigines use primitive weapons to catch animals

Kangaroos are marsupials. The females have a kind of pocket or pouch on their bellies, in which the newly-born babies lie and receive their mothers' milk until they are big enough to find their own food.

Kangaroos are very odd-looking animals. They have very large hind legs made of three equal parts that look like the letter Z. This type of leg makes the kangaroo an excellent jumper.

The tail is long, tapering and heavy. As the kangaroos jump along they use their tails to support their bodies and help them to balance. At each hop the animal can cover a distance of up to 10 metres and kangaroos have been known to travel at 40 kilometres an hour. They use their speed to escape from danger, for they have little else to defend themselves against an enemy except their powerful hind legs which they use to kick hard any attacker.

Where people still live as in prehistoric times

The Stone Age ended about 5,000 years ago, but in some places on the Earth there are tribes and small communities of people who live very much as prehistoric man did.

The Aborigines of Australia are one example. These people have dark, chocolate-brown skins and wavy black hair. They live by hunting and fishing and by gathering wild fruit and honey. The weapons they use to catch animals are primitive, their spears and arrows fitted with stone points.

Aborigine women spend their time looking for vegetable food such as roots and palm nuts because these people know nothing about growing crops or rearing animals. One reason for this backwardness is that Australia is largely a barren and inhospitable land, lacking the plant life necessary for feeding livestock.

Ethnologists, scientists who study the various peoples who inhabit the Earth, estimate there are some 50,000 Aborigines left in Australia. Their degree of development is considered to be about the lowest in the world. But the Aborigine can manage to exist in surroundings that would kill a civilized white man and this capacity for survival is proof that these are intelligent people with great powers to adapt themselves to their surroundings.

One of the reasons why the Aborigines can overcome the many great difficulties they face is their social life. Relationships among the various members of the community are very simple and basic. There are no class distinctions or social classes, no rich and no poor; every Aborigine is on an equal level and they all have the instinct of working together for the good of everybody.

Aborigines express their myths in art, music and dance, the actors painting their bodies with ritual designs.

The boomerang is used by Aborigines when they hunt

Where the boomerang is used

The boomerang, a weapon that is thrown at its target, is used by the Australian Aborigines when they are hunting. If correctly thrown, the boomering returns to its owner if it misses its target. The curving path of the flying boomerang is the result of the shape of this weapon which is made of wood and bent like an elbow, with the edges thinner than the middle.

The boomerang spins as it travels through the air and the Aborigine can vary the spinning movement and the path of the weapon in the way he throws it.

141

Where Koala bears live

The koala is one of the strange animals to be found in Australia. It is a marsupial, the baby koala bears spending the first six months of their lives snug and warm in a pouch attached to their mothers' stomachs, just as baby kangaroos do. Koala bears are as small as mice when they are born, but once they have grown big enough they leave the pouch and climb up on to their mother's back where they stay, hanging on to the fur, until they are fully grown. Koala bears are said to mature at four years old and live to about twenty.

An adult koala is a charming animal that looks rather like a grey-brown teddy bear. It is approximately 60 centimetres long, weighing from 5 to 8 kilogrammes, and lives in eucalyptus trees. The koala bear is very fussy about its food and eats only the aromatic leaves of four varieties of eucalyptus trees out of the hundreds of different kinds that grow in Australia. For this reason koalas cannot be kept outside their natural surroundings.

Koala Bear with a young bear on its back

Where to find 'the land of the many islands'

The easternmost part of Oceania contains thousands of islands, which are scattered about the Pacific Ocean in groups known as archipelagos. This is Polynesia, 'the land of the many islands'.

The islands are distributed throughout the Pacific from the equator to the Tropic of Capricorn. Some of these islands are formed from the hardened lava of volcanoes and rise quite high out of the ocean. Most of them are of coral and are so low and flat that they can only be seen at a close distance. These coral islands are grouped in rings: inside the ring there is a peaceful stretch of water called a lagoon which is protected by the coral barrier formed by the islands.

How did men in early times manage to reach these remote islands, separated from each other by thousands of kilometres? The Polynesians know little about their beginnings: they have no writings and the story of how their distant ancestors first came to the Pacific islands has been passed on by word of mouth so that is has become full of myths.

Studies of the region and its people indicate that Polynesia was first populated by primitive peoples from Asia who moved on to Micronesia. Some sixty dialects are spoken in Polynesia and they all have a gentle, sing-song quality. The best-known are Hawaiian, Samoan and Tahitian.

In the islands that have been least touched by European or Chinese civilization the people have the characteristic build of Polynesia: full lips, full faces and wavy, reddish-brown hair, which the women grow to their waist.

Eucalyptus forest

Where they still use stones to catch fish

In Bora-Bora, a beautiful island in the Iles Sous le Vent, the people still use stones to catch fish in the same way as described by Captain Cook in the early 1700s.

Just before the start of the rainy season, the *tavana*, who is the leader of the fishing expedition, meets with his fellow leaders to organize the hunt. The women on the island begin to weave large fishing nets. The oldest of the *tavana* then asks for the blessing of the gods on the venture.

The fishermen paddle their canoes out to sea and then stop, forming a huge arc, while the women and children wade into the water stretching out their nets. Then each *tavana* takes a stone tied on to the end of a piece of rope and brings it down with a resounding splash on the clear waters. As the canoes race forward, the *tavana* keep hitting the water with their stones and the great ring of canoes gradually closes in. The women and the children cheer the rowers on excitedly; the water boils and froths and the fish, terror-stricken, dart away from the terrible din and straight into the waiting nets where the men spear them.

Where the wild eucalyptus grows

The eucalyptus tree grows in Australia where it is commonly called 'gum tree' or 'stringybark'. There are many varieties including some which are among the tallest trees in the world, rivalling the sequoias of America in height though not in massiveness. Near Melbourne there is a eucalyptus tree that is more than 120 metres high. This tree is exceptional, but many eucalyptus trees grow to more than 80 metres.

In Europe these trees only grow to about 50 metres because of our cooler climate, but even at such a height the tree is a giant. The trees are easy to recognize because of their bluish-green leaves and their graceful trunks.

The leaves are evergreen, long and oval in shape and rather stiff. They have a sharp smell because they contain certain oils used in

Papuan Tree Python

making perfumes and medicines. The wood is durable and pest-resistant and is good for building as well as for burning. The bark provides tannin, a substance used in making leather. Some species yield gum and from others resin is obtained.

Where pythons live in Oceania

Pythons live in Australia and in the island of New Guinea. These snakes grow to a length of more than 4 metres. They have a beautiful skin which is light brown in colour covered in black spots. In other Pacific islands pythons live in rocks. These are known as the amethystine pythons and grow to a length of 6 metres.

Pythons lay leathery-shelled oval eggs, sometimes as many as a hundred, and look after them very carefully. The female python sits on the eggs for about two months, coiling her body like a spring so that she keeps the eggs safe and warm.

With the boas, pythons are the giants in the world of snakes and their huge size is quite frightening. The largest species is the regal python which lives in Malaya and can grow to a length of 10 metres. Pythons are to be feared because they can crush an animal as big as a cow within their coils but although the pressure is considerable, the victim is actually killed by suffocation. They rarely kill anything as large as cattle, however, for they swallow their prey whole and their mouths cannot be stretched much beyond the size of a pig. Like all snakes that constrict, or crush, their victims, pythons are not poisonous and they rarely attack man.

Where the bottle tree grows

The bottle tree is a strange plant that grows in the grassy plains of Australia. It gets its name from the shape of its trunk, which is thick and swollen like a huge flask, narrowing at the top from where the branches grow.

There are many kinds of bottle tree. The most common look like enormous bottles with their very broad bases and narrow necks. The bottle tree is not very useful: it produces no edible fruit and the wood is only fit for burning.

The trunk of the tree consists of

Diamond Python

soft, spongy wood which during the rainy season soaks up the moisture and stores it for use during the dry season. Some bottle trees have been cultivated for ornamental use, especially in southern California and Florida. The name bottle tree (*Brachychiton acerifolium*) is grown especially for its brilliant red flowers that appear during the brief period when the tree is leafless.

Where the fiercest battles of the Pacific were fought

After the Japanese surprise attack on Pearl Harbour on 7 December 1941, the United States declared war against that country and the Pacific Ocean became the scene of many fierce battles. Much of the war was fought at sea; never before had such mighty fleets of warships challenged each other. Thousands of aeroplanes also took part in the fighting.

The most famous naval battle took place off Midway Island between 3 and 6 June 1942 when the Japanese lost four aircraft carriers to the United States' one. The skirmishes that followed around the smaller islands in the Pacific were just as bitter. These battles were often to win possession of a small scrap of land in the middle of the ocean, but small as they were, these places were of vital strategic importance. In the early part of the war the forces of Japan had the advantage and soon won control over the Pacific zone. The Americans tried to win back the lost territory at Guadalcanal, one of the southern Solomon Islands, but this attack showed how difficult it was to fight back from island to island.

The Japanese showed themselves to be fierce, fanatical warriors, ready to die rather than surrender. But in the summer of 1943, when Guadalcanal was won back by the Allies, the slow, remorseless advance of the Americans began, supported by an unrivalled force of arms.

The Marshall Islands, the Philippines, the Marianas, Guam, Leyte, Iwo Jima and Okinawa were the many stages of the reconquest. At Okinawa the Japanese first used a suicide weapon called *baka*. This was a glider loaded with explosives and powered by rockets, which was guided by a pilot who died when the glider crashed on to its target. Victory came only after fierce battles at sea and on the various islands between land forces. The Japanese had to be rooted out from tree to tree, from cave to cave, and thousands of men perished.

145

Emu with its young

Where the male bird hatches the eggs

The emu, the second largest living bird, inhabits the great, semi-arid plains of Australia where it wanders about in small groups through the flat grasslands.

During the mating season the male emu chooses a wife and starts a family with her. The male not only makes the nest, a shallow pit in the ground, but he chases his mate away and sits on the eggs himself.

An emu nest can contain up to fifteen large, blue-green eggs, each weighing about 600 grammes. The hatching period lasts two months and when the baby emus, covered in striped down, are born they are ready to walk about and look for their own food.

The emu has been greatly reduced in numbers and is in danger of dying out. Attempts are being made to breed it domestically for its meat.

Where kava is the national drink

Kava is the national drink of Polynesia. It is made by the *taupo*, the Polynesian word for the most respected girl in the village. This girl is chosen as mistress of ceremonies: she chews the roots of the pepper plant from which the drink is made and prepares the beverage.

First of all a young man fills a large wooden bowl with the chewed kava powder. Then he

Costumes of the Fijian Islands

pours the milk of a coconut over the *taupo*'s fingers and some more of the milk into the kava powder. The *taupo* then moves her hands in accordance with a ritual pattern, stirs the mixture into a paste and strains it through hibiscus. More milk is added; the *taupo* opens her hands and rests them on the edge of the bowl and the drink is ready. Those taking part in the ceremony then clap their hands rhythmically while a cup-bearer fills a cup and raises it to his head. He pours out the yellowish-green contents and the kava is then passed round according to the rank of those present.

Where Australia is richest in water

Australia's only great river is the Murray which flows into the ocean near Adelaide. The valley of the river Murray runs south-west from the Great Dividing Range the southern slopes of which are rich in forests of eucalyptus trees and the home of most of Australia's characteristic animals. Farther to the west the forests give way to broad grassy plains with scattered thickets of acacia trees.

The Murray is 2,550 kilometres long and its main tributary is the river Darling. Along its twisting course the Murray receives the waters of many small rivers and streams. Because of the varying rainfall the Murray does not have a steady rate of flow: it can be reduced to a trickle or suddenly become swollen. Imposing dams have been built to make the river flow in a more regular manner and to exploit its waters. As a result the wastelands around Adelaide and Victoria are giving way to cultivated fields and orchards.

The explorer George Grey, threatened by natives

Where cockatoos live

The cockatoo differs from the parrot in the shape of its beak and the feathers on top of its head. Its beak is smaller than that of a parrot and is also more compressed. On top of its head, the cockatoo has a handsome tuft of feathers which can open out like a fan when the bird is excited or alarmed.

The white cockatoo is easily recognized because of its white plumage, unknown in any other species of parrot. The feathers on the cockatoo's head are a beautiful sulphur-yellow, the only splash of colour on an otherwise completely white body.

This bird lives in large groups on the edges of dense forests in Australia. It prefers open spaces near forests, with light and room to fly, and the forests provide its food which consists of green shoots and tuberous roots. Its nest is usually in a high tree hole where the baby birds, naked and blind when hatched, are fed by the parents for about three months.

These parrots seem to love the sound of their own voices. They also imitate other sounds, including the human voice, and are very clever at repeating phrases which are spoken to them.

Other varieties are the rose-crested and the bare-eyed cockatoos and the galah. The giant black cockatoo with its naked cheeks which go red with excitement, lives in the forests of New Guinea.

Where fish are caught with lassos

The Polynesians regard the shark, especially the man-eating shark, as a kind of god. For this reason shark-hunting in Polynesia is a very ancient ceremony with something sacred about it.

The fishermen put out to sea at dawn, using large canoes with outriggers to keep the vessel stable during the hunt. On the orders of the *tavana*, the leader of the fishermen, the men rattle bells loaded with bait close to the water. This is a very dangerous moment for many fishermen have lost fingers or even a whole hand to the shark.

As everybody keeps a sharp look-out a shadow suddenly appears underneath the water: it is the shark. Some bait is lowered into the sea to draw the fish towards the trap. The fisherman with the lasso waits for the right moment and when it comes he throws the rope round the shark's neck, tightens the noose and then pulls the fish in. The other fishermen then join in and beat the shark to death with heavy clubs as the water turns red with its blood.

The fishermen keep speaking to the shark until it is dead as if the animal understands them. The dead fish is then tied to the outrigger and the islanders spend the rest of the day fishing, followed by huge flocks of gulls.

When the fishermen go back ashore they are so laden that as they reach the shallows of the rocks they have to jump out of their canoes and push them in front of them.

The whole village gathers together to celebrate their return as a triumph of man over the hostile forces of nature.

Rose-crested cockatoo

Galah cockatoo

Giant black cockatoo

Where the cassowary lives

The cassowary is a large, flightless bird, over one and a half metres in height, which resembles the emu. It has long, thick, black plumage; its bare neck is knobbly and its head is also bare and crowned with a peculiar swelling that resembles a helmet.

The cassowary lives in the forests of New Guinea and the nearby islands and the north-eastern tip of Australia. It feeds mainly on fallen fruit and on small animals such as snails, lizards and the chicks of other birds.

These birds live in groups. They are rather timid and wary but are easily detected by the sound of their deep, windy sighs. They run away from any danger and can reach speeds of up to 50 kilometres an hour.

Where to find mammals which have beaks

The duck-billed platypus is the most archaic, or outdated, of all the mammals, more like a reptile or a bird. It lays eggs but when the babies are hatched they live on their mother's milk. Instead of teeth, the platypus has a beak. It lives only in Australia where it has survived to our own day because of that continent's isolation from the rest of the world.

The platypus is an aquatic animal, with webbed feet, rather like a beaver in its habits. It is an excellent swimmer and builds its home in the bank of the river. The entrance, which is under the surface of the water, is a long tunnel that leads to a roomy chamber lined with dry grass. This is where the baby platypuses are born and the mother keeps them in her pouch where they feed on her milk.

The platypus feeds by dredging the muddy bottoms of rivers with its flat beak. It lets the water run out of the sides of the beak and the little animals that live in the river mud are trapped inside its mouth. The platypus immediately stores these animals in roomy pouches in its cheeks and eats them later in the quiet of the riverbank. From time to time the platypus leaves the river and rests on the shore when it eats what it has caught slowly and with great enjoyment.

Platypuses
(*Ornithorincus anatinus*)

The home of the platypus

**Hei-tiki,
a Maori charm**

Where the last of the Maori tribes live

The Maoris are a people of Polynesian origin who moved to New Zealand between about the eleventh and the thirteenth centuries. They brought to South Island agriculture and the arts of weaving and pottery. The Maoris achieved quite a high degree of civilization but they were never able to form themselves into one state. When the Europeans came to New Zealand the Maoris withdrew farther into the interior of the country. According to the 1971 census their number has been reduced to 227,414 scattered throught the northern zones of the island. Intermarriage between Maoris and European New Zealanders is increasing steadily and a growing number of Maoris are moving into the towns.

Maori society was based on an aristocratic structure and ruled by chiefs and priests. The people were divided into three classes: the nobles, the warriors and the slaves. In many tribes cannibalism was practised and human heads were preserved by being smoked.

The traditional dress of the Maori consists of heavy robes made of woven fibres and decorated with kiwi feathers. Their houses are rectangular in shape and the villages are protected by strong palisades. The Maoris are skilful artists and are especially known for their sculptures and wood carvings.

Maori costumes

Where the wild breadfruit tree grows

The first navigators to explore the South Seas and their remote islands found that the natives ate bread although they had never seen wheat. The flour for this bread was obtained from the fruit of a large tree which grows to a height of 12 to 20 metres. The wood of the tree is excellent for making canoes and furniture; the bark provides a fibre that can be woven into material; and glue is obtained from the milky juice that oozes from cuts in the trunk. But the most valuable part of this tree is its fruit which can be harvested three times during the year.

The greenish-brown breadfruit is roundish and from 10 to 20 centimetres in diameter. It has a white, pulpy flesh that can be eaten raw, boiled in water, or even fried or roasted. When the pulp is dried it can be ground into a flour which the islanders use to make small loaves.

Where the wombat lives

The wombat is a largely nocturnal animal that lives in Australia. Like the kangaroo, the wombat is a marsupial, but unlike the kangaroo it does not have a long tail and cannot jump. Wombats look rather like koala bears but they have a pair of sharp, continuously growing incisor teeth on their upper jaw and another pair on the lower jaw so that, like any rabbit or other rodent animal, they have to keep gnawing at hard foods to prevent these teeth from growing too long.

Wombats are vegetarians and eat grasses, the inner bark of shrub and tree roots and occasionally fungi. They use their very strong forefeet to dig tunnels, pushing the soil back with their hindfeet. These tunnels can be up to 3 metres long and a few have been found more than 30 metres long.

The flesh of the wombat is prized locally and these harmless animals have been almost completely wiped out by hunters.

There are two species of wombat: the naked-nosed wombat makes his home in Tasmania and the hilly or mountainous regions of south-eastern Australia; the hairy-nosed group lives only in southern Australia.

Craspedophora magnifica

Where the wonderful dancing birds live

The male bird of paradise is among the most beautiful birds in the world. During the mating season it dances for the female, hopping and hovering on a leafless branch, beating its wings majestically, stretching out its neck and ruffling up its feathers to display plumage of vivid orange, yellow, blue, green, brown and red.

Birds of paradise are quite common in Australia and New Guinea. One of the most beautiful species is the royal bird of paradise, a quick, mischievous creature forever greedy and hungry like a crow.

(*Vombatus hirsutus*) Common wombat

151

THE WHERE OF THE SEAS AND THE OCEANS

Where divers reach their greatest depths

Underwater exploration is almost as old as man himself. There is evidence that primitive man went swimming under the sea although he did not go down as far as divers do today in the search for whatever gifts the depths of the seas have to offer. However, diving under the sea with no breathing equipment and relying simply on holding the breath, was not done to any great extent until the present century. This type of underwater swimming has proved valuable in helping to understand how the human body behaves in such conditions.

One of the most famous divers of this type is Raimond Bucher who in 1952 reached a depth of 39 metres. This was a great feat because this depth is considered the limit of human endurance under water.

In recent years men and women have been able to dive to even greater depths. These have not been as impressive as Bucher's achievement because these divers used special breathing equipment including masks, rubber diving suits, and cylinders containing compressed air which the diver carries on his back and from which he breathes through a mouth-tube. These skin-divers also have flippers on their feet to help them swim faster under the water.

Bucher is also one of the world's greatest skin-divers and has discovered a way of avoiding the painful and dangerous condition which attacks the body if a person comes back to the surface too quickly from deep water. He has carried out over 1,000 dives to a depth of more than 80 metres and even reached depths of about 100 metres.

(left) Modern aqualung equipment including neoprene wet suit, snorkel tube, depth gauge and single compressed air cylinder
(right) Face mask, heavy duty boots and single hose

Lactophrys quadricornis

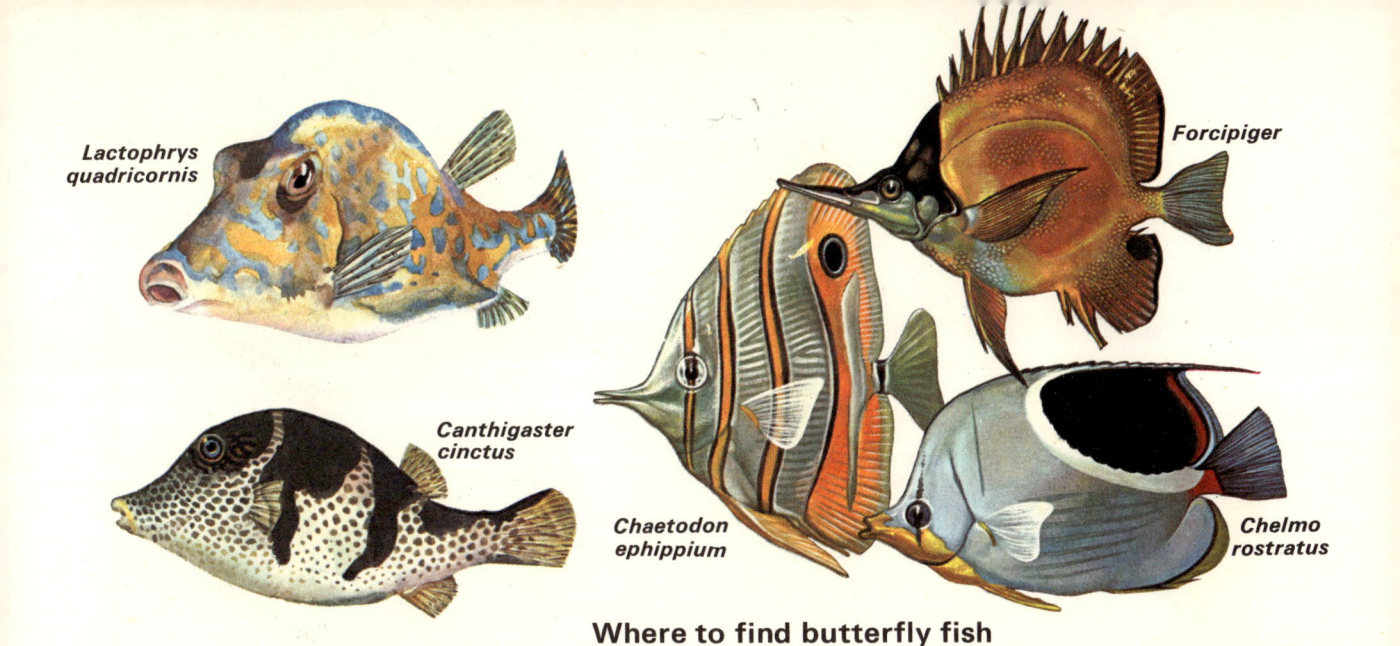

Canthigaster cinctus

Forcipiger

Chaetodon ephippium

Chelmo rostratus

Where the world's largest fish lives

The world's largest known fish is the whale shark which can grow to a length of more than 18 metres and weighs several tons. The whale itself cannot be regarded as fish because it is a mammal that lives in the sea.

The jaws of the whale shark are big enough to swallow a man, but this huge fish is harmless to human beings and lives on plankton, the tiny animal and plant life that floats near the surface of the oceans. The whale shark scoops up the plankton as it swims along and strains it through its rows of small teeth. This shark lives in tropical seas and swims near the surface for most of the time.

To catch a whale shark is a real stroke of luck for fishermen because this is a valuable fish. Every part of its body is used, the flesh as meat and the skin for leather. The liver of the whale shark provides an excellent oil; the Chinese use the dried fins to make a delicious soup; the bones and the entrails produce fertilizer; and the teeth are sold as curios or good-luck charms.

Where to find butterfly fish

Butterfly fish live in tropical seas. They dart swiftly among the coral reefs in shallow waters in large numbers, always ready to hide away in dark rocky corners should danger arise.

It is very difficult to catch a butterfly fish and most fishermen do not bother to try because it is not very good for eating.

The fish's name makes it clear that this is a beautiful creature and the vivid colours make one think of a light-winged butterfly fluttering from flower to flower. These fish are boldly marked with black bands and frequently have eye marks, although no two fish have identical patterns. Their markings together with their brilliant colours, mostly yellows, make them very conspicuous.

The butterfly fish is small, rarely exceeding 20 centimetres, and narrow, like a flounder, but it has enormous fins, often unusual in shape. The mouth is small with bristle-like teeth and the body is covered with rough scales. Baby butterfly fish do not resemble the adults at all: they have no colour on their scales and they have a collar or sheath round the neck, which they lose as they mature.

Where coral grows

Coral needs clear, running water and light, the two indispensable elements of life for the polyps, the small creatures who live in coral. The light stimulates these tiny animals and the running water brings them their food, consisting of bits of plant and animal matter. The sea must also be clean because mud would kill the polyp colony. For this reason, coral is scarcely ever found at the mouths of rivers where mud usually gathers.

When the polyps feed they push out little branch-like tentacles, each containing a tiny bag of stinging liquid which has the same effect as a nettle. When the polyp pushes out all its tentacles it makes a beautiful sight, but as soon as any danger comes along the tentacles are quickly withdrawn.

The colour of corals varies from a bright vermilion red, through pink, to white, due to the presence of iron salts which the calcium of the polyps soaks up.

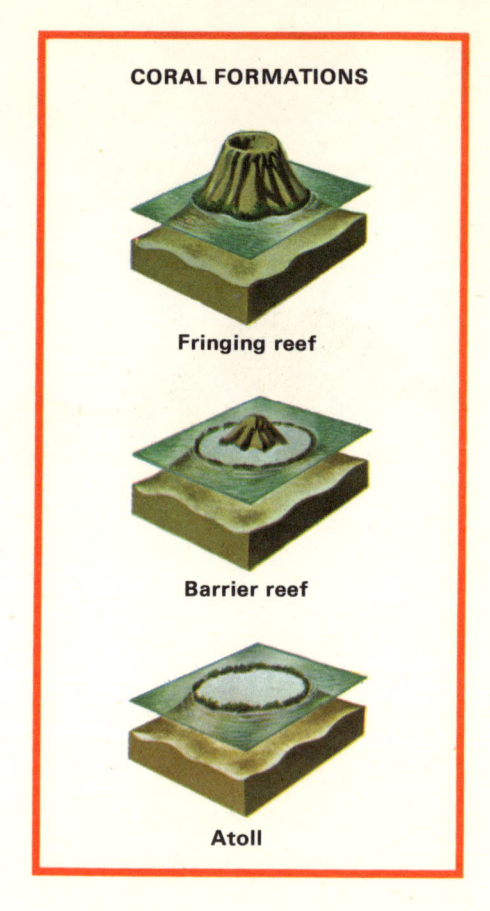

Many coral banks are destroyed by primitive methods of fishing that are sometimes used to bring these beautiful things to the surface. It is difficult for any man to swim down to the depths where fine corals grow so many fishermen use a heavy piece of wood shaped like a cross to which nets are attached. The fishermen drag this piece of wood along the bottom and as the wood strikes against the corals it breaks off pieces which are then caught inside the net. This method of fishing makes it difficult to bring up large pieces of undamaged coral and also does great harm to parts of the coral colony which are still in the process of growing.

CORAL FORMATIONS

Fringing reef

Barrier reef

Atoll

The *Gertruyd* of the Dutch East India Company

Where the road to India lay

The East India Companies that operated during the seventeenth and eighteenth centuries were extremely powerful commercial and political organizations. The most important were the East India Company of Britain and that of Holland, but the French and some other European nations also operated several of these organizations.

These companies did not restrict themselves merely to the exploitation of the rich trade in spices and other eastern products, but formed empires of their own in various parts of Asia.

The swift sailing ships were amongst the most beautiful and the best-armed in the world. Their route to India went by the west coast of Africa and round the Cape of Good Hope, for the Suez Canal was not yet open. After the Cape the ships followed various sea routes to India and Malaysia.

Where to find the great depths of the oceans

The depths of the ocean are much greater than the height of even the tallest mountains. Mount Everest, for instance, is 8,882 metres above sea level while the bottom of the Pacific Trench lies 11,022 metres below the surface of the water. This huge abyss is also known as the Mariana Trench. Another abyss, in the Atlantic Ocean, the Puerto Rico Trench, also known as the Milwaukee Trench, is 9,219 metres deep.

One of the great pioneers in exploring the lower depths of the oceans was Auguste Piccard who in 1953, in his specially built bathyscaph, *Trieste*, went down to a depth of 3,150 metres and to 3,700 metres in 1956. Piccard's son Jacques carried on his father's work and in 1960 he went down into the Mariana Trench to a depth of 10,916 metres.

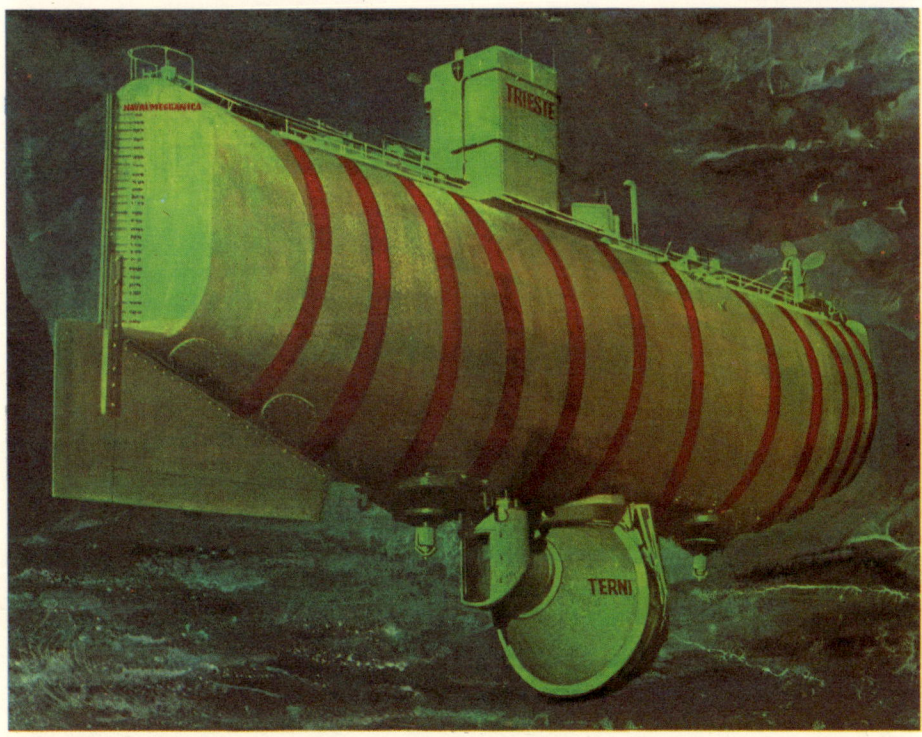

Piccard's *Trieste*

Where the cod islands lie

The cod is a cold-water fish which lives mainly in the north Atlantic, the North Sea and the Baltic Sea, swimming in the open seas at depths of about 300 metres.

The best place for cod fishing is round the Lofoten Islands off the north-west coast of Norway, where more than 5,000 fishing vessels trawl during the fishing season.

Where sea-monsters have been seen

There are many sailors' tales, some highly improbable, about encounters with huge monsters at sea. Recent reports, however, are more exact in their details and reliable witnesses maintain they have seen gigantic sea-monsters emerge from the depths of the sea.

Some scientists believe these creatures could be the last descendants of the enormous sea-dinosaurs which were thought to have died out 70 million years ago.

One of the most sensational encounters with a sea-monster was reported to have taken place in the Pacific Ocean on 13 January 1852. On that day a ship called *Mononghaela* was sailing through calm seas when suddenly, a few hundred metres away, there appeared an enormous beast like a snake. The monster was brownish-green with a huge head and a great fin on its back like that of an eel. The tail was crested and covered in bony knobs.

The sailors could not believe their eyes. Yet the monster was there before them, threshing about in the waves as if it were fighting some other huge animal. Then the master of the ship, Captain Seabury, lowered the boats and the sailors surrounded the animal to riddle it with harpoons. The monster shattered two of the boats into matchwood with powerful blows of its tail before it sank mortally wounded. The next day, with the help of a ship called the *Rebecca Sims*, the sailors recovered the animal and towed it to the shore. The eyewitnesses said it was a huge serpent more than 35 metres long, with a head almost 3 metres long and a body more than 10 metres wide at its thickest point. The huge mouth contained about 100 extremely sharp teeth and the skin was so tough that the sailors could not chop it up with their axes.

The sailors' description of this monster is surprisingly like that which scientists have pieced together from the fossilized remains of sea-dinosaurs.

Diagram of a trawler positioned over a shoal of fish with sound waves being reflected

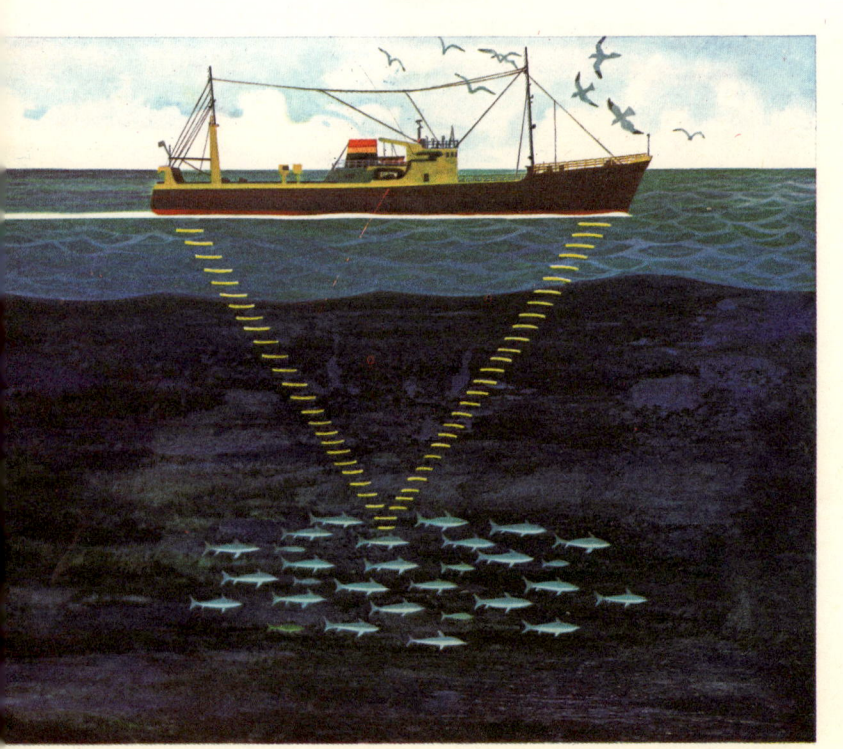

Where oil is extracted from the sea

The demand for oil is growing rapidly. World reserves are gradually becoming less and there is a risk that they will be completely used up. For this reason, scientists are studying other possible sources of power such as atomic power or solar energy.

Until these two sources can be harnessed the search for oil has been extended to the sea. The first oil wells at sea were placed in shallow waters near the coast but gradually these oil wells were built farther away from land and out in the open sea. This has been made possible by special floating platforms which can be anchored even in the ocean in order to drill for oil deposits on the sea-bed. These oil wells have been drilled in such places as the Persian Gulf, the Caribbean Sea, the Adriatic, the Caspian Sea and the North Sea.

Where to find giant clams

Giant clams with shells more than a metre long, live along the coral reefs of the South Seas.

The best-known of the giant clams has the scientific name *Tridacna*. It is composed of two shells, or valves, which are covered in a beautiful glistening substance called mother-of-pearl. The shells are corrugated with wavy edges.

The giant clams anchor them-

Oilfield rigs at Abu Dhabi in the Persian Gulf

selves to coral banks and are fully exposed when the tide goes out. Then the clam keeps its valves tightly closed, but at high tide, when the clam is completely submerged in the water, it opens its valves slightly to filter scraps of food from the water.

Where sponges are gathered

The bath sponges that we use are fished in the Mediterranean Sea and the Atlantic Ocean. They are sea animals that live on rocks in shallow waters near the shore. The part of the sponge that we use is the skeleton of the animal from which the soft body has been removed. Sponges are among the most simple of animals that can feed and reproduce themselves.

There are about 5,000 different kinds of sponges. Their bodies consist of a fleshy mass full of cavities or small holes which are connected with the outside world by means of pores. Through these pores the sponge filters seawater to obtain plankton, the minute animals that float near the surface of the sea and which are the sponge's food.

Where to find some of the world's strangest and ugliest fish

The order of fish known scientifically as Lophiiformes contains some of the strangest creatures in nature, often with such monstrous and bizarre shapes that they seem to have come out of a nightmare. Many of them live in tropical seas or in the farthest depths of the ocean which are the deepest part of the Earth. There are also some in the Mediterranean.

The angler fish is included in this order. It is a delicious fish to eat but so ugly that fishermen have to cut off its head and skin

Porcupinefish

Anglerfish

it before they can sell it. Not many people would like to eat such a monster with a large head and its body covered in prickles, warts and all kinds of knobs. Another ugly feature are the fins which look like legs.

The angler fish grows up to 2 metres long and its head takes up half of the whole body. Because of its enormous head the angler fish is a slow swimmer and prefers to drag itself along the sea-bottom.

Where to find the world's biggest crab

There are many varieties of crab, all interesting creatures because of their habits and instincts which make them the most intelligent members of the crustacean family.

Many crabs are caught as food and one of the most valuable of these is the crab which lives around the British and European coasts. It has a flattened body and a smooth shell which is roughly triangular in shape. From this shell there grow five pairs of legs, the first pair being much larger than the others and ending in pincers.

The biggest member of the crab family lives in the seas around Japan. The legs of this giant are sometimes more than 4 metres long and give it an awkward appearance as it moves along the sea-bed.

Where to find crowds of seagulls

Seagulls are proud and wild birds who spend most of their time in the air, wheeling and turning as they utter their harsh, unmistakable cries. For sailors, the presence of seagulls is a sure sign that land is near.

These birds are beachcombers who rid the shoreline of all sorts of refuse. They are always hungry and very daring in their constant search for food, snatching fish from boats and fishing baskets and going close to houses when bad weather drives them inland.

Where the great ocean currents are formed

Ocean currents are caused by differences in temperature of the water. In the region of the equator the water is warm as it receives the full force of the Sun's heat which comes in rays that run straight down to the surface of the Earth. The rays of the Sun at the equator travel a shorter distance through the Earth's atmosphere than at any other part of the globe and so lose less of their heat.

As the waters of the ocean become warm they expand. The waters around the equator are therefore less dense than those around the polar regions which are much colder. This difference in water temperatures leads to a movement in which the warm water flows out to colder regions and the cold water is pushed towards the warm areas. The speed and direction of these currents is determined by winds and the rotation of the Earth.

Where eels go to lay their eggs

Eels are quite common in the rivers of Europe where they are often caught for their meat. Every year they migrate in large numbers on mysterious journeys to distant waters.

The eel spends most of its life in rivers, although there are also sea-dwelling eels such as the conger and the moray eel. But

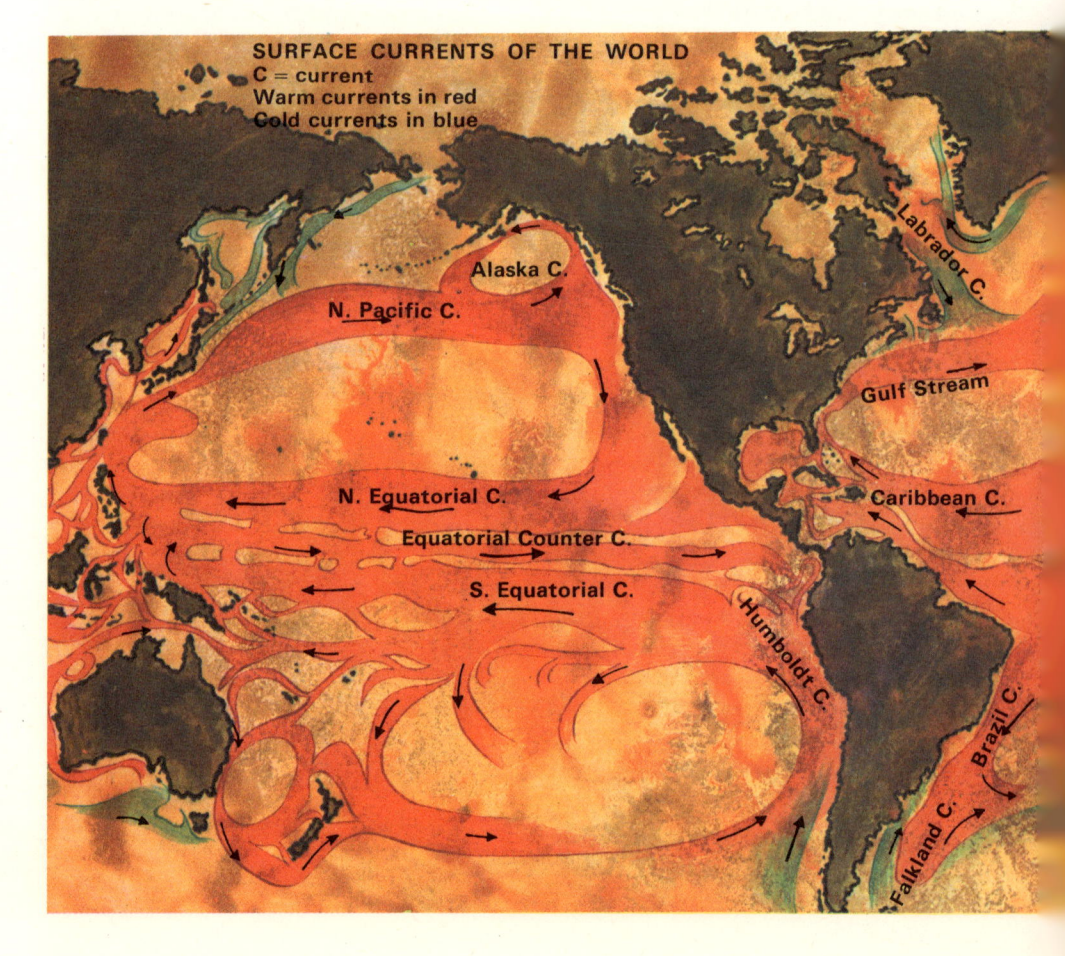

SURFACE CURRENTS OF THE WORLD
C = current
Warm currents in red
Cold currents in blue

when the time comes for these snake-like fish to lay their eggs they leave their streams and rivers and head for the open sea. For thousands of kilometres they swim along until they reach their destination which is the Sargasso Sea in the western Atlantic.

The baby eels are born in the Sargasso Sea. About two and a half years later these young eels, known as elvers, are back in the rivers and streams of Europe. They stay there for about fifteen years until they are adults. Then they feel the call of the sea and set out on their long journey.

Scientists have put forward many possible answers to why the eels swim all the way to the Sargasso Sea to lay their eggs but so far it still remains a mystery.

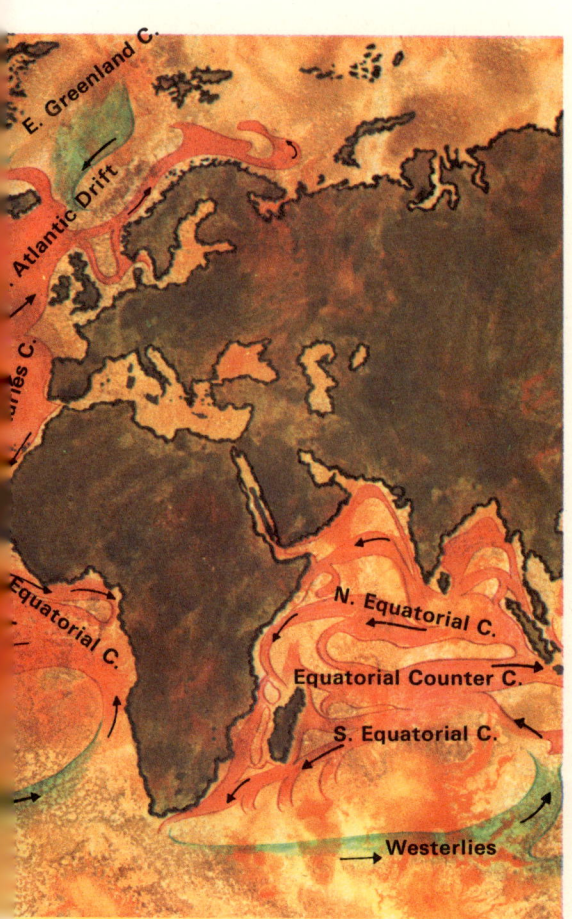

Where man-eating and harmless species of sharks are found

The word 'shark' always conjures up the picture of a very fierce, dangerous, man-eating fish. In actual fact, sharks which attack people are few and many species of shark live near coasts presenting no threat or danger to human life. Some sharks are quite small including varieties in the Mediterranean which are caught because they are very good to eat.

The sharks which are most dangerous to man live in warm seas. These include the terrible white shark which is 12 metres long and attacks seals, sea turtles, large fish and occasionally man. Other sharks involved in attacks on humans are the tiger, the blue, the grey nurse and the hammerhead.

Along certain stretches of the Australian coast the danger from sharks is so great that beach-guards keep a look-out for them and shout warnings through loudspeakers to bathers. A shark's presence in the sea is announced by its tall, sail-like fin sticking up through the water.

THE WHERE OF THE POLAR REGIONS

Where the Eskimos live

Modern anthropologists believe the Eskimos first came from central Asia during the last great Ice Age. In their appearance, Eskimos resemble Mongoloid peoples who live in eastern Asia: their skin is a pale yellow, their hair is straight and black, they have dark, slanted eyes and high cheekbones. Eskimos are stocky in build and have broad chests although their hands and feet are small. One feature in the Eskimo which is different from the Mongoloid face is the nose which is quite long and narrow.

The Eskimos are probably all descended from the same group of people because their way of life throughout the regions they inhabit is the same. They are divided into tribes scattered over vast areas of the northern polar regions and this makes it impossible for there to be complete contacts among all the various tribes. But the Eskimos all share a similar way of life. Their customs, clothes, the tools they use to hunt and fish, their methods of catching animals and their social organization are all the same whether in Siberia or northern America.

Most Eskimos live around the shores of the Arctic Ocean and on the eastern and western coasts of Greenland. Eskimos also live on the Labrador coast, round Baffin Bay and in the far north of Canada.

In all there are about 5,000 Eskimos and it is thought that they never numbered more than that. Their language is very complex and few foreigners have learned to speak it fluently; in Alaska even the Eskimos are beginning to simplify it. The people are very hardy and are able to endure the rigours of the ice and snow which last from six to nine months of the year.

Where to find elks

The elk, which is called the moose in America, is the largest animal member of the deer family and lives in marshy regions and forests of the far north. The male, or bull, elk is a majestic-looking animal both in its size and the shape of its enormous antlers. A fully grown elk is more than 2 metres tall at its shoulders and can weigh up to 700 kilogrammes.

The male elk sheds its antlers every year in autumn. They grow again in the spring and in a fully-grown animal the antlers have about twelve points. The female elk, or cow, is smaller than the bull and has no antlers. The elk likes to live in open marshy areas where it wanders in search of grazing grounds. It also eats leaves, the bark of trees and water-plants.

Because of their antlers and large size, elks are sought as trophies by hunters. They are also killed for their meat, which is rather like beef. Their numbers have been greatly reduced by hunting and they are now usually protected by law.

Where the caribou lives

In the far north of the American continent, above the sixtieth parallel, lives the caribou, a grass-eating animal that is a close relation to the reindeer. The caribou is also known as the woodland reindeer and is quite common in northern forests.

During the summer it roams north, feeding on moss, lichens and the other few forms of plant life that grow in those regions. In winter, caribou gather together in large herds and migrate south to search for their food. In former days this was the time when the animal was hunted and many of them were slaughtered. In the first half of this century over-hunting reduced their numbers from nearly 2 million to 200,000.

There are two main kinds of caribou: the barren-ground caribou that lives in wastelands, and the larger woodland species that makes its home in woods. Caribou that live in the Arctic belong to the first group. These animals are not easily domesticated but for the Eskimos they are a vital source of meat, wool and skins for making clothes. The reduction in their numbers caused serious problems for some inland Eskimos who had to be moved to different areas to avoid starvation.

Eskimo costumes

Where the polar bear lives

The polar bear is a large beast of prey which lives amid the ice-floes inside the Arctic Circle. Nature has been generous with this large animal: it has given it a thick, white fur which enables the bear to stand up to extreme cold; a very fine sense of smell which helps it know where its prey is, even at a very great distance; and such enormous strength that it can knock down a strong man with a single blow of its paw.

The polar bear has great cunning and has completely mastered the art of moving across the ice, approaching its victim silently from behind. It seldom goes without food, therefore, even though it lives in cold and barren places. The bear's favourite victims are seals, but it will also snatch salmon and other fish out of rivers with its paws. This animal swims very well and is often found many kilometres from land or ice packs. It has been known to follow migrating seals as far south as the Gulf of the St. Lawrence in America.

Where the polar pack ice forms

The vast stretches of ice around the polar regions present one of the most impressive spectacles in the world. After the very short polar summer season the wind begins to blow and snow covers the ground as far as the eye can see. Great packs of ice form which spread out over the ocean, joining together the mainland and islands into one solid white mass. As the pack ice rests on the sea it cracks in places and moves about in the current.

This inhospitable world which has remained largely unexplored for thousands of years, is the home of the Eskimos, a people who can stand up amazingly to biting cold, hunger and exhaustion. It is difficult to understand how the ancestors of these people chose such an icy and cold place to live in and such hostile surroundings.

There is one theory that the Eskimos are descended from Stone Age peoples who became used to living and hunting in the ice during the great Ice Age. When the ice melted and retreated to the north, the animals that lived on it also went northwards. The hunting tribes therefore decided to follow what had become their only source of livelihood and they moved to the north too.

Where igloos are built

The Eskimo home that is best-known is the igloo although it is not the most commonly used dwelling place of these people. The igloo is built only in the far north of the Canadian Arctic and is always a temporary home. About three-quarters of the Eskimos have never built an igloo.

Home for an Eskimo is a snug chamber dug out of the ground and covered with pieces of wood. The cracks in the wood are sealed with dried moss and lichens.

The igloo is only a shelter for anyone travelling or hunting. It can be built in half an hour or even less by cutting blocks of snow with a large knife and placing them on top of each other to form a dome-shaped house. The entrance is through a long tunnel, dug in the snow, and this helps to keep the warmth inside the igloo. Animal skins are placed on the floor and light comes from a lamp which burns oil extracted from seals' meat. It is warm in the igloo even when the temperature outside is 50° below zero.

Where the huge prehistoric mammoths lived

The remains of mammoths, which lived about 100,000 years ago and were related to present-day elephants, have been found in quite large numbers in Siberia where the vast plains between the glaciers in the north and the forests in the south provided ideal surroundings for them.

Mammoths were well protected against the cold for their bodies were covered in thick, woolly fur. They were big, powerful animals and few other creatures dared to attack them, so they lived quite peacefully grazing on the plains or feeding on leaves. Some of these huge animals were still living when man first appeared on the planet.

165

Wolves

Where to see the aurora polaris

One of the most unusual natural happenings to be seen in the skies are the aurora polaris which light up the heavens above the North or the South Poles. These auroras are called the northern lights or aurora borealis ('northern dawn') when they take place in the northern hemisphere and the aurora australis when they occur in the southern hemisphere.

The northern lights are the better-known of the two. They can sometimes be seen as far south as the Mediterranean, but they display their full majesty inside the Arctic Circle.

It is difficult to describe this great wonder of nature. Some auroras simply bathe the night sky with a serene milky light just above the horizon. Others consist of rather sinister colours like flickering flames, haloes of light, bright, hanging curtains or arcs or mysterious shapes that ripple and wave in the air.

For hundreds of years all sorts of fables and legends grew around these lights. As with most great natural phenomena, many people thought they were some sort of warnings from another world.

Today astronomers know that these strange and beautiful lights in the polar regions are caused by magnetic storms. These storms send out charged particles which travel to the Earth's poles. When they collide with the Earth's atmosphere the particles glow. The lights are often green though they are occasionally pink and yellow. The auroras take place about twenty-four hours after the passage of a sunspot across the Sun.

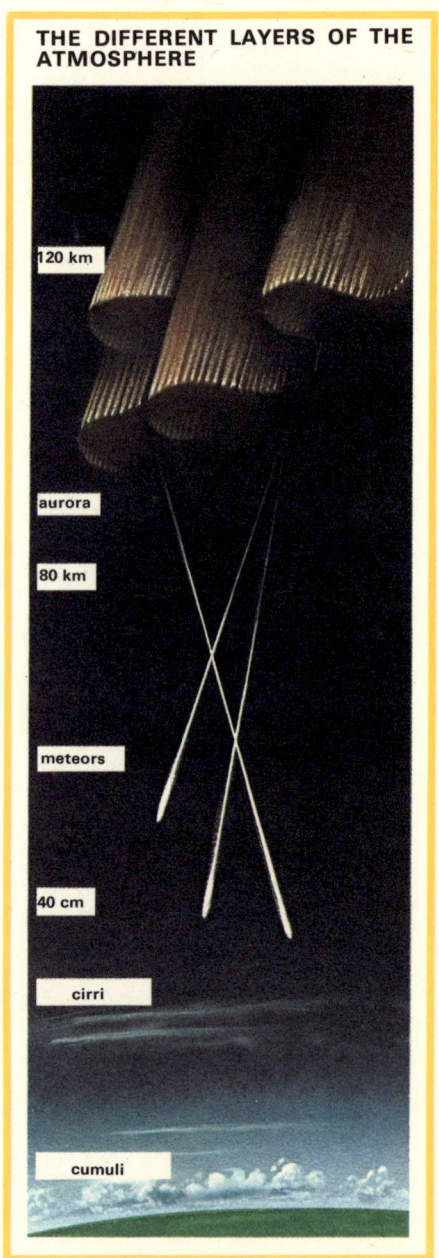

THE DIFFERENT LAYERS OF THE ATMOSPHERE

120 km

aurora

80 km

meteors

40 cm

cirri

cumuli

Where wolves are plentiful

Wolves have disappeared from most regions inhabited by man but they still live in packs in the tundra, the barren plains of the Arctic, where they present a constant threat to other animals.

They are powerful creatures, often measuring over 2 metres long, including the bushy tail, and the only animals who can stand up to them are the musk oxen which always live together in big herds. When wolves attack them the oxen stand shoulder-to-shoulder in a huge ring with their horns pointed outwards.

The musk ox is a stubborn fighter and the wolf knows it and prefers to attack something less dangerous such as foxes, hares, lemmings and other mammals, only rarely hunting large animals such as reindeer or caribou.

Where to admire the midnight Sun

The North Cape is a rocky promontory north of the Scandinavian peninsula. The water round it does not freeze in winter because it is near the warm current of the Gulf Stream. Every year thousands of tourists flock here to see one of the most impressive and extraordinary sights: the midnight Sun.

Night and day at the North Pole coincide with the seasons. Day, for example, lasts about sixty-five days and coincides with the summer. The Sun never rises high in the sky, it is never too bright and it seems to move very slowly. Towards the evening it begins to set until it reaches the horizon when it appears to hesitate. This happens at midnight.

Then, very slowly, the Sun begins to climb again in the opposite direction. This phenomena depends on the angle of the axis of the Earth. When the Earth is at its summer solstice, the Sun shines on the North Pole. The Earth is tilted in such a way that the Sun never sets even though the Earth is going round and night and day take place in other parts of the globe.

Aurora polaris

The different shapes and colours of the aurora polaris

167

Where the people of the frozen north find the material for their clothes

The Eskimos' clothes are all made from animal skins or furs. The leather is made by the women of the tribe from the skins of polar bears, reindeer, foxes and seals. The dress of an Eskimo consists of a short coat with soft fur lining, trousers made of caribou skin or polar bear fur and long, woollen leggings, like socks, with the fur turned inside. These leggings are also stuffed with dried grass and moss to keep them snug and warm. With them Eskimos sometimes wear a type of boot which is usually made of sealskin because it is not spoilt by dampness.

In the depths of winter the Eskimos put on two of everything, the inner garment with the furry side against the body and the outer with the fur on the outside. Between the two garments there is a layer of air that acts as insulation and keeps the body's warmth from escaping. This double layer of clothes weighs little more than 5 kilogrammes and allows the Eskimo to move quite freely.

Snowy owl and lemming

Where the lemmings migrate

The snow-lemming is a rodent that lives in the Arctic north. Another species of lemming lives farther south and is well known because of its mysterious mass migrations. Huge flocks of these animals suddenly start running from the mountains of Norway and do not stop until they reach the coast where they plunge to death over the cliffs into the sea. This mass suicide is thought to occur when the lemming population becomes too high and there is not enough food to feed them all.

Where the explorer Vitus Jonassen Bering died

Vitus Bering was a Danish-Russian explorer who was born in 1681. He served under the Tsar of Russia as leader of an expedition to see exactly how the continents of Asia and America were separated. Bering set out from Kamchatka in eastern Asia in 1728. He travelled north and reached St Lawrence Island where he was able to prove without the shadow of a doubt that the two continents were separated by a stretch of water which, at its narrowest, is about 90 kilometres wide and about 45 metres deep. This stretch of water was named the Bering Strait after the explorer.

In a later expedition, Bering carried out a careful examination of the northernmost coastline of the American continent. This expedition began in 1741 and ended tragically. Bering was forced to go ashore by the severe storms at sea. He landed on an island off the coast of Kamchatka (the island was later named after Bering) and died of scurvy on 19 December 1742. Many members of his expedition also lost their lives but a small group succeeded in escaping by building a rough boat.

Where birds go to in the Arctic

Birds fly where they will and are not limited by boundaries. They can be found as far as the North Pole in summer. Many birds go on migrations that take them thousands of kilometres in order to lay and hatch their eggs in the north during the short Arctic summer.

North American snipe

The golden plover is one of these. The plovers arrive in the Arctic in spring. They have beautiful blackish-brown plumage scattered with golden yellow triangular spots; in the autumn these colours fade. Perhaps, if the plover stayed on in the Arctic in winter, its feathers might turn as white as the snow, as happens with the ptarmigan (snow partridge), but the plover is a migratory bird and when winter comes, it flies south.

The golden plover holds the world record for making the longest flight without coming to earth for a rest. It can fly from Alaska to Hawaii, a distance of over 4,000 kilometres across the Pacific Ocean.

Golden plover

Liverwort
(*Pellia epiphylla*)

Lichens
(*Leptogium*)

Puffin
(*Fratercula artica*)

Where plants still grow in the far north

It seems impossible but even amid the icy wastes of the Arctic there are plants that grow, flower and reproduce themselves. They grow wherever the land thaws, even if it is only for a few days in the year.

These plants are small and stand up to the cold. Their life cycle is very short but they still represent a triumph of life over the great difficulties presented by the Arctic.

In some Arctic zones the only plant life known are the lichens. Lichens are really pioneer plants, even tougher than mosses, and can take root on rocks. As they hook themselves on to the bare rocks these plants produce an acid which gradually corrodes the rock so that small pieces of it constantly fall away. These minute particles, together with the remains of dead lichens, provide a fertile base on which higher forms of plant life can grow.

Lichens are unique in being a combination of plants from entirely different groups, a fungus and a type of seaweed. These two forms of plant life combine their qualities into one plant that can survive in difficult conditions.

Mosses are also common in the tundra. These mosses grow in large expanses which are enlivened here and there by splashes of colour from heather which become green during the summer. When winter comes the heather grows dry and tough, but grass-eating animals still look for them because when food is scarce these plants can provide a meal.

Also fairly common in the Arctic are plants of the *Carex* family which form yellowish clumps that turn green in the spring thaw. These plants include the saxifrages and a few snow-poppies.

Where to find puffins

The puffin, also known as the sea parrot or bottlenose, is a seabird that is very common along the northern coasts of Canada and Alaska, in Iceland and in northern Scandinavia.

A puffin can be recognized by its very odd beak which is high and flattened at the sides and is covered in yellow, blue, orange and red stripes. Puffins live in large colonies on island cliffs or on rocks where they build a strange nest which is more like a burrow because puffins dig out long tunnels in the ground. They also use burrows that have been abandoned by rabbits. They lay their eggs in a little cave about 2 metres under the ground.

Puffins feed mainly on fish and can catch as many as ten small fish in succession, carrying them dangling across their beaks to their young.

Where dogs still pull sledges

Today civilization has reached the polar regions and explorers travel on powerful vehicles fitted with caterpillar tracks to move over the snow and ice. But sledges pulled by dogs are still the most sure form of transport through the icy wastes and, for the Eskimos, these sledges are a necessary means of survival. Without them contacts between the scattered villages would be impossible and it would also be very difficult to go hunting for food.

Eskimos use almost any material for making sledges. When wood is scarce, bits of old plank or any other flotsam washed up by the sea is used; sometimes the antlers of a reindeer are turned into a sledge; the frozen skin of a seal is often used or simply a piece of deep-frozen meat.

The sledge is pulled by a team of dogs known as huskies, incredibly tough animals able to stand up to the terrible cold, hunger and exhaustion. They are faithful and valuable friends to man when he is out hunting and have an excellent sense of smell which can detect the presence of game birds at great distances.

Huskies can pull a sledge along at more than 30 kilometres an hour for up to eighteen hours at a stretch. When the Eskimos feed their dogs they are always careful to serve the leader of the sledge team first so that it retains the respect of the other dogs.

The sledge is mostly used for carrying goods such as fish for the dogs, provisions and clothes for the Eskimo and hunting weapons. The Eskimo goes on foot steering the sledge from behind, and wearing skis or snow-shoes when the snow underfoot allows it.

Where seals take their ease

Several varieties of seal live in the Arctic and although they differ in shape and size, they all share a similar way of life. These animals are all superb swimmers, able to lie still for hours in the water and then rush off at incredible speed.

Seals often sleep in the water, letting the waves gently rock them to and fro. They can dive down to great depths but have to come up to the surface often in order to breathe. Their main food is fish, but they will also accept any other small sea-creature.

On land and on the ice they

171

move very clumsily dragging themselves along with their flippers. They never stray too far from the water and are ready to dive into the sea at the slightest sign of danger. Their hearing and sight are very sharp but this does not prevent them from being frequently caught and killed by polar bears.

Where to find the Strait of Magellan

The Portuguese navigator Ferdinand Magellan left from Spain on 20 September 1519, with five ships and sailed all round the coast of South America including its southernmost tip.

Magellan also explored the stretches of water that separate Patagonia from the mainland. He found there a bleak and desolate land which seemed uninhabited by day, but when night fell the sky was lit up by scores of fires which the natives had lit as an alarm signal. Magellan called the region 'Tierra del Fuego' which is Spanish for 'the land of fire'.

Having discovered the strait that was later named after him, the great navigator sailed through it. After enduring terrible storms and overcoming the most severe hardships he came to a huge expanse of ocean. To the sailors who had come through such an ordeal this ocean seemed very calm so they called it the Pacific, which means 'peaceful'.

Magellan continued his journey to the north, sailing along the coast of Chile, and then westward and eventually reached the Philippine islands. On 27 April 1521, he went ashore on one of these islands and was killed in a fight with natives. Of the five ships that set out only one returned, and of the original crews only eighteen men saw their homeland again; but these men were able to claim they were the first to have sailed round the world.

Where penguins live

Penguins are flightless birds that live only in the southern hemisphere. They have become so well adapted to their life in the sea that they are among the best swimmers in the southern oceans. The first explorers and travellers to visit the Antarctic regions were amazed when they first saw penguins which look as if they are wearing male evening dress of white tie and tails and walk along in a funny, stiff manner that makes them seem quite pompous.

These birds live in large colonies along beaches and the early travellers thought them to be extremely intelligent creatures by the way they laid and hatched their eggs and found food for their chicks in a strictly organized manner. But what the penguin shows is not so much intelligence as a perfect adaptation to sea life. Their bodies are streamlined; their feathers are like small scales and their wings have become like flippers.

Penguins only come ashore during the breeding season when as many as 40,000 of them will crowd together on the same island, although they are not really social animals and are individuals by nature.

Some species of penguins migrate and others stay in the same place. When there is no danger about they are lively and happy creatures: they love to hop about, dive in the sea and spin round on their toes, barking and making lowing sounds and filling deserted bays with their noise.

Where the walrus lives

The walrus was known several hundreds of years ago but accounts of this animal were few and vague. The first accurate descriptions came with the early polar expeditions. The explorers who came across herds of these animals found them a good source of food for themselves and their dogs which pulled the sledges. Walruses are massive animals: the males are much larger than the females, reaching a length of up to 4 metres long and weighing more than a ton.

Though big, the walrus is a peaceful and lazy animal. It lives in large herds on rocky banks and on ice sheets along the shores. When walruses are not sleeping they go for a swim in the icy cold sea, usually keeping to comparatively shallow water

Ringed Penguin and Gentoo Penguin looking for fish

and digging out clams from the seabed. They are often hunted for the excellent ivory in their tusks, for their very tough skin, and for the oil which can be extracted from their blubber.

Adelie Penguin

173

Where blue whales were hunted

The blue whale is the largest animal in the world. The enormous size of this sea-dwelling mammal made it an extremely valuable catch for a whaling ship. The blue whale, which weighs 150 tons and measures up to 30 metres in length, provided a large range of valuable products which were extracted on the factory ship that processed these animals on the seas of the polar regions.

A very strange thing about the blue whale is how such a huge animal manages to live on tiny, shrimp-like creatures which are no more than 5 centimetres long. The whale eats about 3 tons of the small creatures every twenty-four hours, catching them by swimming through the sea with its jaws open. It uses a bony sieve hanging from the roof of its mouth, known as the baleen, to strain its food from the water.

Today there are very few blue whales left for over-fishing has brought this animal close to extinction. Since 1966 the hunting of blue whales in the southern hemisphere has been prohibited by international agreements.

Where the limit to human habitation lies in the southern hemisphere

The fifty-fifth parallel in the southern hemisphere crosses the southern tip of the island of Tierra del Fuego. This line marks the last regions to be inhabited by people living in the desolate regions of the south.

The islands of Tierra del Fuego were discovered in 1520 by Ferdinand Magellan who gave them their name. The islands lie at the southernmost tip of South America and consist of one large island, known as Isla Grande, a few smaller ones and many tiny islets.

The climate in this region is unfriendly. Often the mountain glaciers send long fingers of ice down to as far as the sea. In the northern islands of the group some plant life manages to grow; there are also forests and broad grassy pastures where cattle and sheep are reared. Some 10,000 people live in this region. The forests, livestock-breeding and deposits of coal and oil provide them with work. Most of these people are of European, Argentinian and Chilean origin: they went there during the last century, attracted by the sheep farming and the discovery of gold and other minerals.

Sperm Whale
(*Physeter catodon*)

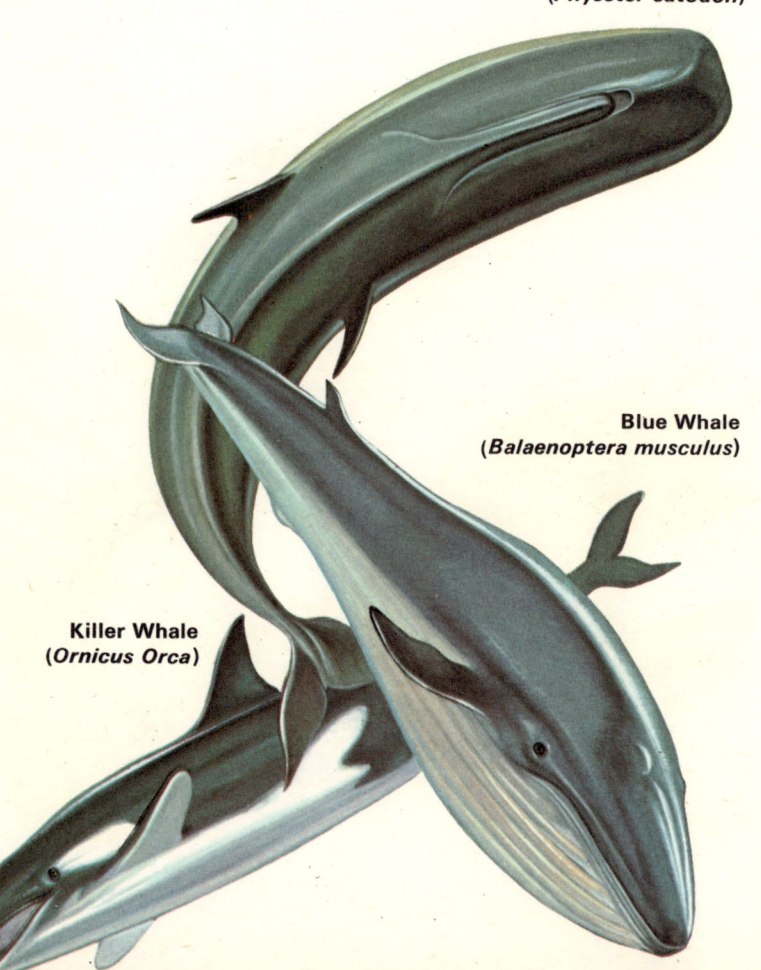

Blue Whale
(*Balaenoptera musculus*)

Killer Whale
(*Ornicus Orca*)

Where the killer whale lives

The killer whale is the biggest member of the dolphin family, growing to a length of up to 10 metres and weighing several tons. It is black with white underparts and white splashes over the eye and on the back, and has a very high, triangular back fin. This whale lives in practically every sea throughout the world but is most common in the cold sea of the polar regions.

The killer whale is one of the most dangerous animals of the Antarctic. It is always hungry and very daring, attacking any other animal it meets. Its targets include fish, porpoises, molluscs, penguins and seals. Sometimes it even attacks whales, tiring them out by frequent and sudden attacks. This aggression has given rise to many legends about the killer whale. Sailors in olden times feared it and believed that this animal was strong enough to capsize their ships or upset ice floes on which men were standing.

Where to find the Ross Ice Shelf

The Ross Ice Shelf is an enormous wall of ice whose sides rise sheer out of the sea to more than 80 metres off the coast of Antarctica. It is a huge floating peninsula which covers about 400,000 square kilometres of the Ross Sea which was discovered by the British polar explorer, Sir James Clark Ross in 1841. It presents a most impressive sight: huge icebergs detach themselves from the wall of ice and are carried away by the current.

This barrier is an insurmountable obstacle to any vessel and ships exploring the region have always had to seek another, less difficult route to unload men and materials. The ice comes from the heart of the continent which lies under incredibly thick glaciers. Streams of ice move slowly down the slopes from these glaciers and merge slowly into one another to form one huge mass which is pushed on into the sea by the pressure of the great ice caps at the centre of Antarctica.

Charles Darwin at Tierra del Fuego

Where the Fuegans of the far south live

Tierra del Fuego is a region in the far south of the American continent which is now inhabited almost completely by people of European, Argentinian and Chilean origin. The native Indians, have been reduced to a few hundred as a result of the settlement of their lands by the whites and the diseases which they brought.

These Indians are known as Fuegans and were once a sea people who lived by fishing. There were also land tribes who reared livestock. Today the Fuegans still live in rough, domed huts made of branches and animal skins. Despite the cold weather they wear scarcely any clothes, covering themselves with rough, sealskin cloaks and mocassins with leggings. They rear a few animals and feed on fish, root plants, grasses and berries. They do not have a very high level of culture.

Where the sea elephant lives

The sea elephant is a giant seal (also called the elephant seal) which lives in the Antarctic. The other species of this animal occurs along the Pacific coast. A fully grown male can grow to a length of 7 metres and can weigh more than 3 tons.

Apart from its large size, the sea elephant gets its name from the trunk-like nose which the males have. This trunk is about 40 centimetres long and dangles down over the animal's mouth.

These large animals are very agile once they get into the water and can defend themselves well against other creatures, but on land they are extremely clumsy in their movements and will put up with all sorts of attacks without hitting back.

Until the end of the last century sea elephants were excessively hunted for their oil. Today they number about 700,000.

Patagonian Indians

Where the Magellan cormorant lives

As its name indicates the Magellan cormorant was first seen in the region around the Strait of Magellan and on the islands near Cape Horn. This cormorant also lives farther north in southern Patagonia, in Chile and in the Falkland Islands.

There are other kinds of cormorant living in the Antarctic regions. These cormorants have blue eyes and resemble the Magellan cormorant although they do not have a red head like the latter. There is also the Kerguelen cormorant, that builds its nest in the Kerguelen Islands, and the royal cormorant. This last bird is perhaps the most beautiful, with a tuft of feathers which grow on its head like a crown.

All cormorants have a long, hook-tipped bill, a small throat pouch and patches of bare skin on the face. They are strong underwater swimmers.

Where the researches of the International Geophysical Year took place

International Geophysical Year lasted from July 1957 until December 1959. It was originally planned for the first eighteen months of this period, but was extended for an extra year. During this time a world-wide programme of geophysical research was carried out. More than seventy nations took part, many of them sending missions to Antarctica. It was on this continent that the most important experiments were carried out, which aimed at obtaining a better understanding of the structure of the Earth. Some of the research stations set up at the time are still manned and have become permanent bases during the summer for scientists tackling the unsolved mysteries of this continent.

During International Geophysical Year Sir Vivian Fuchs crossed Antarctica from the Weddell Sea to the Ross Sea. At about the same time, Sir Edmund Hillary, the conqueror of Everest, reached the South Pole, arriving shortly before Fuchs.

LIST OF QUESTIONS

Where you can find the most densely populated state	10	Where you can find the home of the bagpipes	19
Where shrews live	10	Where you can find the fish which produce caviar	20
Where you can find the cork-oak tree	10	Where you can find forests full of beech trees	20
Where you can find the land of fiords	11	Where the edelweiss grows	20
Where you can find Megalithic monuments	11	Where you can find a land full of windmills	21
Where the boar lives	12	Where you can find the most famous city on water	22
Where flying began	12	Where you can find important Etruscan cemeteries	22
Where you find the home of the mouflons	12	Where you can find beautiful marble	23
Where you can find the Alhambra	13	Where you can find the land of the sunflower	23
Where you can find the friezes from the Parthenon	13	Where you can find the remains of ancient human settlements in Northern Europe	24
Where the Victorian style was born and flourished	14	Where you can find the most famous natural grottoes in Europe	24
Where the horned viper lives	14	Where Palladio's art is supreme	25
Where you can find the vauclusian spring	14	Where sleighs are still being used as taxis	25
Where the sacred mistletoe ceremonies were held	15	Where the Neanderthal Man used to live	26
Where you can find the land of the tulips	16	Where orchids grow in Europe	26
Where the lynx was seen again in Europe	16	Where you can find the most important atomic centres in Europe	27
Where you can find the valley of the temples	17	Where you can still find seals in the Mediterranean	27
Where you can find the smallest state in the world	17	Where you can find the land of lakes	28
Where the brown bear lives	18	Where you can find the famous	
Where you can find crocodiles in Europe	18		
Where the ancient town of Spina once stood	19		

valley of the roses	28
Where there exist many relics of ancient Roman life	29
Where you can find the island of fire	29
Where the wild cat still lives in Europe	30
Where you can find a town made of salt	30
Where fox hunting is a national sport	31
Where you can find invaluable remains of Greek civilization	31
Where the water in oases of the Sahara desert comes from	32
Where the desert rat lives	32
Where the cheetah hunts its prey	33
Where savanna plant life grows	33
Where to find dome-shaped huts	34
Where great herds of zebu are reared	34
Where to find wild peacocks	35
Where the world's largest ape makes its home	36
Where the optical illusion of mirages occurs	36
Where the ships of ancient Egypt sailed on their voyages of discovery	37
Where to find Africa's largest national parks	38
Where to find the Victoria Falls	38
Where the cola used in making soft drinks comes from	39
Where to find the bird that snakes fear	39
Where the religious festival of Ramadan is celebrated	40
Where to find 'the traveller's tree'	41
Where Africa's chief Moslem centres are located	41
Where the ancient Egyptians obtained papyrus	42
Where the desert viper lives	42
Where Stanley and Livingstone met	43
Where the crowned crane lives	44
Where the nomads of northern Africa roam	44
Where the salt road passes through the Sahara	45
Where trees defy the sea	46
Where raffia comes from	46
Where the Nile rises	46
Where Africa's chief mineral deposits lie	47
Where the desert nomads pitch their tents	48
Where the pygmies live	48
Where termites are found	49
Where the Hausa live	49
Where the Kei apple grows	50
Where the world's largest tree grows	50
Where the Masai live	51
Where the okapi lives	51
Where to find negroes who have never been influenced by white people	52
Where the great civilizations of Africa flourished	52

181

Where the most terrible of the locust plagues take place	54
Where geraniums first came from	54
Where man's earliest ancestors lived	55
Where the evil-smelling *Rafflesia* flourishes	56
Where the raw material for strychnine is produced	56
Where the armies of Alexander the Great marched	56
Where the 'Roof of the World' is located	57
Where the elephants of Asia live	58
Where camphor comes from	58
Where to find the most beautiful city in Japan	58
Where the city of Troy stood	59
Where the art of *ikebana* and bonsai was born	60
Where ginger is produced	60
Where the pheasant first came from	61
Where the Great Wall of China was built	61
Where the Ainu live	62
Where the most beautiful gentian in the world grows	62
Where rice is more important than wheat	63
Where to find gibbons	64
Where bonzes live	64
Where the first atomic bomb fell	65
Where to find the 'waters that purify'	66
Where nutmegs come from	66
Where to find the people who have always been at war	67
Where the Phoenician civilization flourished	68
Where the monsoon winds blow	68
Where to find the 'Venice of the East'	69
Where the Bedouin live	70
Where the emperors are regarded as divine	70
Where lychees grow	71
Where to find the yurts of the Mongolians	71
Where to find teak	72
Where the persimmon came from	72
Where the tiger likes to make its home	73
Where jute, kapok and ramie are found	73
Where birds help to keep the streets clean	74
Where bananas first grew	74
Where hamsters come from	75
Where to find the earthquake islands	75
Where to find the sacred gavial	76
Where to find the salt-water crocodile	76
Where the mango grows	76
Where cormorants help fishermen	77
Where to find the pangolin	78
Where the dugong lives	78
Where opium is grown	78

Where to find the sacred volcano	79
Where to find the Chinese alligator	79
Where the Kurds live	80
Where the fig is held sacred	80
Where the Baluchi live	80
Where to find the archerfish	81
Where the fur hunters of America tracked their prey	82
Where to find the world's most famous waterfalls	82
Where the winged lizards lived	82
Where to find the most majestic valley in the world	83
Where to find the world's tallest trees	84
Where chewing gum comes from	84
Where to find the main Indian reservations	85
Where to find poisonous snakes that are helpful to man	86
Where some of the earliest reptiles appeared	86
Where the big cattle trails crossed the American prairies	87
Where the first fossilized remains of the horned dinosaur were found	88
Where the giant cactus grows	88
Where the burrowing owl lives	89
Where to find the main space control centre of the United States	89
Where the first inhabited centre of New York arose	90
Where sisal is produced	90
Where to find the most famous geyser in America	91
Where to find the glass palace of the United Nations	91
Where America's biggest river flows	92
Where alligators live	93
Where the swamp cypress grows	93
Where the magnolia trees come from	94
Where to find the national park of the Everglades	94
Where to find the Cape Canaveral launching pad	95
Where bison live	96
Where the main battles between the Indians and the whites took place	96
Where the first inhabitants of America came from	98
Where gold fever broke out in the Wild West	98
Where to find the siren	99
Where the first Europeans landed in America	99
Where the pioneer trails to the west were made	100
Where the trail of the legendary Pony Express ran	100
Where the Pacific Railroad began	101
Where to find America's most ancient human settlements	102
Where to find the legendary Fort Alamo	102

Where Columbus landed	103	in the Andes mountains	114
Where the ring-tail cat lives	103	Where sweet potatoes come from	115
Where the civilization of the ancient American Pueblo Indians flourished	104	Where to find the world's highest lake	115
Where the cashew grows	104	Where the straw is produced for Panama hats	116
Where to find Death Valley	105	Where the quinine tree grows wild	116
Where the Mayas lived	105	Where to find the famous ruins of Machu Picchu	117
Where philodendrons come from	106	Where to find the world's most beautiful orchids	118
Where liquidambar for perfume is produced	106	Where the peccary lives	118
Where to find the huge dams of Tennessee	106	Where the opossum lives	118
Where the capital of the Aztecs was situated	107	Where to find the country with the fewest roads	119
Where to find the world's largest forest	108	Where the brightly coloured macaw lives	120
Where the first fuchsia plants were found	109	Where the first potatoes were discovered	120
Where to find the world's highest railways	109	Where the Brazil nut grows	120
Where to find the world's highest capital city	110	Where the jaguar lurks	121
Where the world's most famous carnival takes place	110	Where to find the splendid bay of the River Plate	122
Where the monkey puzzle tree comes from	111	Where the pawpaw grows	122
Where alpacas are reared	111	Where manioc is eaten	122
Where the terrible piranha fish lives	112	Where head-hunters live	123
Where to find the world's biggest estuary	112	Where maté is the national drink	124
Where the guava comes from	112	Where to find avocado plants	124
Where arrowroot is produced	113	Where the rubber tree grows wild	124
Where American monkeys live	114	Where the condor lives	125
Where to find the highest peak		Where to find the cold waters of the Humboldt current	125
		Where they build houses for	

snakes	126	on his voyages of exploration	138
Where the giant *Megatherium* lived millions of years ago	126	Where to find the flying phalanger	138
Where to find the great petrol lake	127	Where sheep graze by the million	139
Where to find the immense 'green sea' of the Americas	127	Where to find the Australian anteater	139
Where armadillos live	128	Where the kangaroo is hunted	140
Where the shells of the glyptodons were found	128	Where people still live as in prehistoric times	140
Where the *burití* race takes place	129	Where the boomerang is used	141
Where to find the longest road in the world	129	Where Koala bears live	142
Where to find pigeons that 'suckle' their young	130	Where to find 'the land of many islands'	142
Where to find the main religious centre of Polynesia	130	Where they still use stones to catch fish	143
Where budgerigars come from	131	Where the wild eucalyptus grows	143
Where to find black swans	132	Where pythons live in Oceania	144
Where to find mammals that lay eggs	132	Where the bottle tree grows	144
Where to find the great deserts of Australia	133	Where the fiercest battles of the Pacific were fought	145
Where to find kangaroos that climb trees	134	Where the male bird hatches the eggs	146
Where rabbits are a public menace	134	Where kava is the national drink	146
Where to find Australia's richest mines	135	Where Australia is richest in water	147
Where the screw pine grows	136	Where cockatoos live	147
Where to find Australia's main cities	136	Where fish are caught with lassos	148
Where to find frilled lizards	137	Where the cassowary lives	149
Where to find the only bird with a strong sense of smell	137	Where to find mammals which have beaks	149
Where Captain Cook travelled		Where the last of the Maori tribes live	150
		Where the wild breadfruit tree grows	150

Where the wombat lives	151	Where the huge prehistoric mammoths lived	165
Where the wonderful dancing birds live	151	Where to see the aurora polaris	166
Where divers reach their greatest depths	152	Where wolves are plentiful	167
Where the world's largest fish lives	153	Where to admire the midnight Sun	167
Where to find butterfly fish	153	Where the people of the frozen north find the material for their clothes	168
Where coral grows	154		
Where the road to India lay	155	Where the lemmings migrate	168
Where to find the great depths of the oceans	155	Where the explorer Vitus Jonassen Bering died	169
Where the cod islands lie	156	Where birds go to in the Arctic	169
Where sea-monsters have been seen	156	Where plants still grow in the far north	170
Where oil is extracted from the sea	157	Where to find puffins	170
Where to find giant clams	157	Where dogs still pull sledges	171
Where sponges are gathered	158	Where seals take their ease	171
Where to find some of the world's strangest and ugliest fish	158	Where to find the Strait of Magellan	172
		Where penguins live	172
Where to find the world's biggest crab	159	Where the walrus lives	173
		Where blue whales were hunted	174
Where to find crowds of seagulls	159	Where the limit to human habitation lies in the southern hemisphere	174
Where the great ocean currents are formed	160		
		Where the killer whale lives	175
Where eels go to lay their eggs	160	Where to find the Ross Ice Shelf	175
Where man-eating and harmless species of sharks are found	161	Where the Fuegans of the far south live	176
Where the Eskimos live	162	Where the sea elephant lives	176
Where to find elks	163	Where the Magellan cormorant lives	177
Where the caribou lives	163		
Where the polar bear lives	164	Where the researches of the International Geophysical Year took place	177
Where the polar pack ice forms	164		
Where igloos are built	165		

The illustrations in this book are the work of the following artists:
D. Andrews, J. Baker, H. Barnett, M. Battersby, J. Beswick, R. S. Coventry, G. Davies, Design Bureau, Design Practitioners Ltd., D. Forrest, G. J. Gallsworthy, R. Geary, G. Green, H. Green, J. Hayes, N. W. Hearn, V. Ibbett, K. Lilly, D. MacDougal, A. McBride, M. McGuinness, B. Melling, P. Morter, J. Nicholls, W. Nickless, D. Nockels, A. Oxenham, J. Parker, D. Pratt, J. Rignall, B. Robertshaw, M. Shoebridge, J. Smith, K. Thole, G. Thompson, P. Thornley, C. Tora, R. Wardel, D. A. Warner, P. Warner, Whitecroft Designs Ltd., M. Whittlesea, J. W. Wood, E. Wrigley.